MAKING SENSE OF
SUICIDE

MAKING SENSE OF
SUICIDE

AN IN-DEPTH LOOK AT WHY PEOPLE KILL THEMSELVES

David Lester, PhD

THE CHARLES PRESS, PUBLISHERS
PHILADELPHIA

The Charles Press, Publishers
Post Office Box 15715
Philadelphia, PA 19103
(215) 545-8933
(215) 545-8937 Telefax
ChsPrsPub@aol.com

Library of Congress Cataloging-in-Publication Data

Lester, David, 1942-
  Making sense of suicide: an in-depth look at why people kill themselves
      p. cm.
  Includes bibliographical references and index.
  ISBN 0-914783-82-3 (alk. paper)
  1. Suicide. 2. Suicidal Behavior. 3. Suicide — Prevention.
HV6545.L419 1997   97-10780
362.28'7—dc21   CIP

  Printed in the United States of America

  ISBN 0-914783-82-3

Preface

The eighth leading cause of death in the United States, suicide prematurely ends the lives of more than 30,000 people a year. For certain groups, the statistics are nothing less than alarming. In the past four decades, the suicide rate has tripled for young men and doubled for young women; it is the third leading cause of death for 15- to 24-year-olds. For young African American males, the suicide rate has veered sharply upward in the last 15 years, increasing by a frightening 358 percent. The situation is even worse when we take into consideration the fact that there are approximately 50 to 100 suicide attempts for every completed suicide, and this obviously does not include the many suicide attempts that are never reported. So ubiquitous is the impulse to commit suicide that one out of every two Americans has at some time considered, threatened, or actually attempted suicide. Finally, we also know that the actual statistics are really much higher than those that are officially documented; many, many suicidal deaths are misrepresented as accidental deaths — both deliberately and unintentionally — and we cannot even begin to estimate the number of people who have seriously contemplated suicide without ever telling anyone. Furthermore, suicide never takes only its intended victim; death by suicide often affects surviving families and friends in a way that is more difficult, more complicated and more intense than the grief experienced from other causes of death.

The high rate of suicidal behavior is doubly disturbing when we take into account that suicide can be viewed as a direct index of the level of unhappiness and psychological dysfunction that exists in the world today. Most people do not resort to suicide unless their lives are so unbearable, unless they are suffering so intensely, that, for them, death is preferable to life.

In light of this, we should be concerned not only with understanding and preventing suicide, but also with improving the quality of life that causes such intense unhappiness. Preventing a person from committing suicide is not necessarily a beneficent act if it means that the person has to continue living a life that he hates. One thing that we know for certain is that suicide is almost always the result of several problematic issues that accumulate over time and result in a crisis situation. It most cases, suicide cannot simply be classified as the act of a "crazy" person or the behavior of someone who doesn't know what he's doing; it is most often a carefully planned out and decisive action, and although others may view suicide as an irrational and illogical behavior, the motivation behind it — usually the termination of a highly painful situation — is usually rational and sound.

Even though the suicidal person usually cannot see an alternative way to end his suffering other than taking his own life, there is almost always a way to resolve or alleviate at least some of his pain. It is true that for some people in certain circumstances (for example, a terminally ill person who is in great pain), death might actually be the best and only bearable way to end their suffering. However, the majority of people do have other alternatives — they just can't see them. Chances are good that with help most people could find relief and maybe even renewed happiness without having to kill themselves.

Due in part to the recent media attention that has been given to suicide, people, both fascinated and horrified by the subject, are finally asking questions: Do we know why people kill themselves? Can we tell that a person is suicidal? Is suicide preventable? What is being done and has it worked? The main goal of this book is to increase general awareness and understanding of the factors that can lead to suicide so that the unnecessary loss of life can be prevented. Unfortunately, suicide is an extremely difficult subject to study for several reasons. Research into behavior is always complicated, but the study of suicide is especially so because, among other things, we obviously cannot talk to a person who has killed himself. We must rely instead on the subjective reports of others and these are often incorrect or clouded by personal opinions and beliefs. Also, it is hard to even define suicidal behavior. There are many types of behavior that can be categorized as suicidal: attempts, threats, thoughts, preoccupations, gestures, attempts that do not involve real intent to die and, of course, completed suicide. Consider, for example, the following three cases of death by suicide:

- An elderly man dies after shooting himself.
- A teenager dies after jumping out a window.
- A woman dies after taking 20 aspirin tablets.

The fact that each of these deaths was classified as suicide does not necessarily mean that the behaviors and the thought processes that led up to the behavior were in any way similar. For example, did they all want to die? How much did they want to die? What were their reasons for wanting or not wanting to die? For all we know, the old man was suffering terribly from a terminal illness and made a rational decision to end his pain by killing himself. Perhaps the woman was simply trying to make her husband see how unhappy she was and never intended to die. Perhaps the teenager was schizophrenic and delusional and didn't know what he was doing. Clearly we must take into account much more than the final result.

This brings us to another confusing issue: the intent to die. Even though a person may intend to die, he may survive. Conversely, a person who intends to survive his suicide attempt may accidentally die. In other words, we cannot always be sure whether a person who has killed himself really wanted to die. In fact, suicide is always a gamble. Even though suicidal people cannot know what death is like, they risk disappointment and hope for triumph or contentment rather than remaining in their present state. This element of ambivalence about death is crucial. The probability that death will occur varies depending on the lethality of the method chosen, but even the most lethal methods are never 100 percent certain to do the trick. The shotgun in the mouth may jam; the fall from a window may be broken by a tree; the poison may not have been correctly labeled. The choice of method, time and place are all indications of a person's degree of intent to die, for they determine the probability that death will occur.

Finally, our investigation of suicide is further hampered because of the problems of conducting controlled research. Assembling the necessary control group of nonsuicidal people presents special problems because subjects may be reluctant to admit that they have acted suicidally or had suicidal thoughts. As well, it is very hard to match the experimental and control groups on all relevant vari-

ables. For example, when we try to determine why a person committed suicide, we must have a group of people who match the
suicide in every way, but who are completely nonsuicidal (i.e.,
imagine the difficulty of assembling a control group of 24-year-old
black males who are twice divorced, now married, but in the process of yet another divorce, with two children — one of whom is
disabled, from an impoverished rural town in the South, who is a
factory worker on the verge of being fired, who has a history of
manic depression, but who has never considered or even thought
about suicide!). We also run into trouble when we try to assemble
the experimental group: because the suicide subjects are now deceased, studies must be conducted on the group that most resembles
them — suicide attempters. But this substitution presents problems
because suicide attempters might be extremely different from completers.

As a result of the complex nature of suicidal behavior, the difficulties of research and the ambivalence of the suicidal person, research on suicide is often criticized, as are the interpretations that
researchers draw from specific results. Throughout the book, I have
tried to synthesize and untangle the often complex and confusing
research reports in order to present only the most salient information. As well, in many cases I have offered criticism of the research.
The reader, too, should keep an open and critical mind and is encouraged to examine the original research reports, the sources of
which are listed in the references at the end of each chapter.

Despite all of the difficulties of research and our inability to come
to concrete conclusions regarding certain aspects of suicide, we have
been able to ascertain quite a lot of information about suicide as a
human behavior. For example, we know that men complete suicide
more often than women; that women attempt suicide more often
than men; that elderly people and young people commit suicide
more often than other age groups; that unemployment is consistently associated with suicide; that suicide is more common in people
who are psychiatrically disturbed; and that depression, especially
the feeling of hopelessness, appears to be the strongest predictor of
suicide. We know also that suicide is not a mysterious affliction that
exists in a vacuum; for most people, suicide is the end result of a
combination of events and it is usually preceded by observable behaviors and warning signs.

In most cases, suicide can be prevented. While it is true that
some people give no warning that they are suicidal, the vast major-

ity of people do. Awareness of the significance of these warnings and knowledge of how to respond to them could mean the difference between life and death. It is therefore clear that the best means of prevention is education. Over the years, a great number of suicide prevention programs have been established that incorporate a variety of strategies. Most of these organizations try to educate the public about suicide and offer assistance to people in a suicidal crisis. And research continues. Despite these efforts, the suicide rate remains high, and for certain groups, it keeps climbing. In light of this, it is more urgent than ever that we continue to intensify our efforts toward understanding this tragic behavior. It is hoped that this book will lend a hand.

A note on the text. For readers who are not familiar with psychological and sociological research, let me offer one word of explanation. In reporting the results of a study, I sometimes say that there was or there was not a "significant" difference between numbers. This expression does not mean that the researchers decided on their own whether or not the results were important. Statistical significance means that the results would occur accidentally only on rare occasions, in other words, 5 percent or less of the time. (However, we must all remember that those rare occasions sometimes happen!)

David Lester, PhD

Contents

1

Suicide: A Meaningful Behavior

- A 50-year-old man, George J., is despondent after losing his job. His wife criticizes him for his inability to make a living and threatens to leave him. He is also concerned about his declining health. One afternoon he goes into the garage, cleans his shotgun, carefully closes the garage door and shoots himself in the head. He dies instantly.

Most everyone would agree that this death was clearly a case of suicide. It appears to fit the dictionary definition of suicide as the act or instance of voluntarily or intentionally taking one's own life.

- A 30-year-old woman, Martha S., learns that she is ill and has only a few years to live. She is unmarried and her mother, to whom she was devoted, has recently died; now she is all alone. She goes to her car in the garage, runs a hose from the exhaust pipe into the window, gets in and starts the engine. Then she takes a handful of sleeping pills. Just as she is losing consciousness, the meter reader enters Martha's garage on his way to her basement. He pulls her out of the car and calls an ambulance. Martha S. does not die.

- A married woman of 25, Susan G., is annoyed with her husband's behavior and decides to teach him a lesson. He arrives home every evening punctually at 5 p.m. At 4:30 she takes a large number of sleeping pills and lies down in the hallway near the front door of their house. The husband is injured in a traffic accident on his way home and he does not come home until late that night. Susan G. dies.

Which of these women has more in common with George J.? Martha S., who fully intended to die but who lived because she was accidentally discovered or Susan G., who ended up dying even though she only wanted to frighten her husband?

1

By looking at these last two cases, we can see that death caused by one's own voluntary act is not necessarily a sufficient criterion to use when judging whether the *psychological* process of suicide has occurred. The woman who meant only to frighten her husband took the sleeping pills "voluntarily and intentionally," and her act resulted in her death. This is, however, not the same kind of psychological process implied in "taking one's own life voluntarily and intentionally." In fact, this particular case of self-destruction seems to be an accidental death following an act that was intended to be dramatic rather than fatal. The only thing that Susan G. has in common with the first case described is the fact that she died.

Martha S., who did not die, actually appears to have more in common with George J. than Susan G. does. Martha and George had histories of recent loss and were threatened with further unhappiness in the future. They both made specific and careful preparations for their deaths, and they used relatively lethal methods. Only an accident prevented Martha from achieving death like George.

These cases make it clear that we cannot understand the suicide process simply by looking at the end result of the actions taken. In the same way, we cannot assume that certain life circumstances invariably cause suicidal acts. Many persons who find themselves in situations similar to George's and Martha's do not behave suicidally. Some people kill themselves because they are disturbed about an event that would not upset other people. The process that leads to suicide cannot be determined by looking at whether death actually occurred, nor by investigating whether a person's life was objectively miserable. Rather, we must examine the purpose of the suicidal act within the pattern of the individual's life.

In newspapers, suicide is often described with statements such as "suicide strikes 30,000 people in the course of a year," or "suicide is the third most common killer of young people." The implications of these descriptions are misleading. Suicide does not "strike" in the sense that measles and tuberculosis strike. Suicide is the result of a gradual process that unfolds within an individual; it is not the work of a mysterious external agency. The "suicide strikes" idea relieves people of the idea that others can sometimes be responsible for a person's suicide. It implies that suicide cannot be predicted and prevented, that people who commit suicide are incomprehensibly struck with the need or desire to kill themselves. We know that this is not true; suicide is a gradual process and, in most cases, persons with suicidal thoughts give many clues regarding their state of mind. Also, as I will demonstrate later, suicide is far more likely to occur in some kinds of people than in others. To understand suicidal behavior and deal with it successfully, we must abandon the comfortable "suicide strikes" philosophy and examine the characteristics of suicidal people.

Just about everyone has a general theory about suicide, but, perhaps because most people simply don't know very much about the subject and have never given it a great deal of thought, they often have a lot of misperceptions. Other people believe that it's pointless, if not impossible, to analyze or theorize about suicide — another belief that generally stems from lack of knowledge. Unfortunately, many of the beliefs about suicide are wrong and, worse, they can be detrimental when dealing with a suicidal person. The following is a list of myths and facts about suicide:

MYTH: People who talk about suicide don't commit suicide.

FACT: Eight out of 10 people who kill themselves give definite warnings of their suicidal intentions. People who make suicide threats and attempts *must* be taken seriously.

MYTH: Suicide happens without warning.

FACT: Studies reveal that the suicidal person gives many clues and warnings regarding his suicidal intentions. Alertness to these cries for help may prevent suicidal behavior.

MYTH: Suicidal people are fully intent on dying.

FACT: Most suicidal people are undecided, often right up until the last minute, about living or dying, and they "gamble with death," leaving it up to others to save them. Few people attempt to commit suicide without first letting others know how they are feeling. This cry for help is often given in code. If recognized, these distress signals can be used to save lives.

MYTH: Once people are suicidal, they are suicidal for the rest of their lives.

FACT: Fortunately, most individuals who wish to kill themselves are suicidal for only a limited period of time. If they are saved from self-destruction, they can go on to lead meaningful lives.

MYTH: Improvement following a suicidal crisis means that the risk of suicide is over.

FACT: Most suicides occur within three months after the onset of a period of "improvement," when people have the energy to turn their suicidal thoughts and feelings into action. Relatives and physicians should be especially vigilant during this period.

MYTH: Suicide occurs more frequently among certain classes of people, i.e., the rich or poor.

FACT: Suicide is neither the rich man's disease nor the poor man's curse. Showing no class prejudice, suicide is represented proportionately in all strata of society.

MYTH: Suicide is inherited or "runs in a family" (i.e., it is genetically determined).

FACT: Suicide does not run in families, and no "suicide gene" has been identified.

MYTH: Suicidal individuals are mentally ill, and suicide is always the act of a psychotic person.

FACT: Studies of hundreds of genuine suicide notes indicate that although most suicidal people are extremely unhappy, they are not necessarily mentally ill. Their overpowering unhappiness may result from a severe emotional upset, a long and painful illness, or a temporary loss of hope.

MYTH: Talking about suicide may give someone the idea.

FACT: Discussing the subject of suicide without shock or disapproval with a person who seems seriously depressed shows that you are taking him seriously and responding to his pain.

MYTH: There are far more homicides than suicides.

FACT: In fact, there are twice as many suicides as homicides in the United States. Suicide is the ninth leading cause of death among adults in the United States and the third leading cause of death among 18 to 24 year olds.

MYTH: If a person really wants to kill himself, no one has the right to stop him.

FACT: Just because a suicide implies voluntary action, that does not mean that the person really wants to die. More often than not, a suicidal person simply wants to escape from pain and even though he may not realize this, death is not the only answer. Chances are the person does not have to die for the pain to stop.

Shneidman and his colleagues (1965) have suggested that there are four principal situations that give rise to a "suicidal crisis," which is a period during which people seriously consider suicide because they feel that the pressures of life have become intolerable. The suicidal crisis may pass, but while present it is a very dangerous period of time. There are four main kinds of suicidal crisis:

1. Impulsive suicidal behavior may follow anger, disappointment or frustration. The emotional crisis may be only temporary, but for an impulsive person it could be extremely dangerous.

2. The feeling that life is no longer worth living may be the result of a serious depression and may lead to suicidal behavior. When a person feels this way he does not understand or believe that his feelings of worthlessness (regarding both himself and the world) will eventually go away. He may feel that he is seeing life as it really is, and in the periods of time when he was not depressed, he was simply deluded about what life really had to offer.

3. Very serious illness may cause people to commit suicide so they can escape suffering. They may also want to kill themselves so they can spare loved ones from the difficulties of caregiving during a long terminal illness. It should be noted that in some cases, the suicidal person may not really be ill at all, but may believe that he is. As long as the belief is present, whether it is true or not, such persons may turn to suicide.

4. Some people attempt suicide in an attempt to communicate or make a statement, but they do not really want to die. An example of this is Susan G., mentioned in the beginning of this chapter, whose death occurred by accident when she attempted to "communicate" her annoyance to her husband. This kind of suicide attempt may be a way to punish others or to win their

sympathy and get their attention. Sometimes, however, it has the opposite result, causing feelings of hostility and guilt in the people close to the attempter. Those who attempt suicide as a means of communication should not be ignored or looked down on because they are "only trying to get attention." Their lives have to be very unhappy for them to be forced to take such desperate measures. And as with Susan G., there is absolutely the chance that they will die as a result of their attempt to "communicate."

CLUES TO SUICIDE

Later in this book I will examine the life situations (such as marital status and age) that can affect a person's chance of committing suicide. Again, suicide does not happen suddenly; it is the result of a gradual process. Suicidal behavior is detectable and most people give specific indications that they are suicidal. While some people make direct verbal statements to this effect, more often than not you can also determine their general mood by their behavior and in the circumstances of their life. The single most effective way to prevent suicide is to learn how to recognize the signs that someone is at risk. The following is a list of behavioral changes that should be viewed as warning signs:

- Suicidal ideation, discussion of suicide and preparation for death
- Depression, hopelessness and irritability
- Substance abuse (both alcohol and drugs)
- Change in behavior (eating, sleeping, attention to personal appearance)
- Changes in appetite (weight loss or gain)
- Loss of interest in sex
- Changes in sleeping patterns, from sleeping all day to not sleeping at all
- Loss of energy and a general feeling of apathy
- Changes from extreme depression to being "at peace"
- Loss of interest in usual activities
- Withdrawing from friends and family

- Making negative comments about himself

- Major change in work or school performance

The following is a list of typical statements that a suicidal person might make (Shneidman, Farberow and Leonard, 1965):

"My family would be better off without me."

"I'm going to end it all; I can't stand this anymore."

"I won't be around much longer, so you won't have to put up with me."

"I don't want to be a burden."

"This is the last straw; this is all I needed."

"I can't stand it any longer: I want to die."

Of course, people who are not suicidal may make comments like these. However, if a sick, unhappy or depressed person makes remarks of this kind, it is a possible sign that he is thinking about suicide. After a suicide has occurred, relatives armed with hindsight may recall many remarks that foreshadowed the death. They may then say that "of course, we couldn't have known he really meant it" but those who are alert and sensitive and who know the facts about suicidal behavior can recognize clues about suicidal intentions and intervene before it is too late.

The following is a list of life circumstances that can significantly increase a person's risk of suicide:

- Recent distressing frustrations, disappointments or losses

- Loss or disruption of normal social support networks (divorce, unemployment, migration)

- Recent stressful life events (death of a loved one, loss of employment)

- Exposure to suicide or suicidal behavior by another person (most common for teenagers and young adults)

- Ready accessibility of firearms (most frequently used method)

- Serious illness or belief that one is seriously ill

- Changes in close relationships

- A history of attempted suicide

- Making a will, arranging insurance policies, cleaning up personal and business affairs

- Giving away cherished or needed possessions
- Previous suicides in the family

Exhibited individually, none of these acts necessarily implies suicidal intentions; many people have wills and life insurance. However, when combined with other suicidal indications — if a person has been ill or depressed, if he has talked about death or taking a prolonged leave of absence, if he seems to be making arrangements for someone else to care for his family when he is gone — then these behaviors may well indicate that suicide is about to occur.

RESEARCH INTO SUICIDE

It is clear that many clues can help identify the suicidal person before he commits the fatal act. (Recollection of these clues after a death can also help establish that the death was due to suicide rather than accident or homicide.) However, suicide assumes many different forms and can be extremely difficult to classify. This complication makes the study of suicide very problematic. Before we attempt to discuss particular areas in which research has given us some understanding of suicide, it might be well to speak briefly about the difficulties of studying suicidal behavior.

Not all suicidal acts result in death. Attempted (nonfatal) suicides and completed (fatal) suicides should be regarded as different forms of behavior. (However, as was noted earlier, an intended suicide attempt or an intended suicide completion may accidentally turn into its opposite.) In addition, there are other, milder forms of suicidal behavior, such as threats or thoughts of suicide.

The most valuable way of categorizing suicidal behavior involves measuring the level of the person's intent to die. Unfortunately, however, measurement of intent is usually very difficult, particularly if the person under investigation is already dead. One problem is that low intelligence or mental disturbance may render the individual unable to achieve his intent. The degree of awareness behind the suicidal act may be an important dimension. It is sometimes claimed that certain people decide to kill themselves in an "automatized" state (as when they have already taken a lot of sleeping pills); in other words, that they are not really conscious of their suicidal intent. Some researchers also feel that serious suicidal preoccupation can lead to automobile or other accidents in which the person is hurt or killed without a conscious intention. Other researchers classify long-term self-destructive behaviors, such as alcoholism, as unconscious suicide attempts. These issues make the study of suicide difficult because if a person is not aware that he is hastening his death, how can a researcher correctly classify the behavior as suicidal or accidental?

Occasionally, individuals who kill themselves may be motivated by urges other than self-destructive ones. Males seeking an auto-erotic thrill sometimes hang themselves briefly in order to cut off their oxygen supply just long enough to achieve sexual orgasm. Quite a few cases have been reported of persons who died in this way (Resnick, 1972). Their motives were undoubtedly complex and probably should not be classified simply as suicidal.

When suicide is studied demographically rather than through individual cases, difficulties may arise because of incorrect classification of cause of death by coroners or physicians. Many social pressures cause the suicide's family to prefer that the death be listed as accidental rather than suicidal. Suicide is still sometimes considered the result of mental derangement or an indication of moral degeneration. Some religious groups will not grant full religious burial privileges to those who have committed suicide. When a death is caused by suicide, insurance companies may only pay back premiums on policies that have been taken out at least two years before the death occurs. In contrast, they may pay double indemnity if the cause of death is listed as accidental. Thus, because many deaths that are caused by suicide are classified as accidental, correct measurement of suicide rates is difficult. Research is further complicated because certain kinds of people are more likely to have their deaths classified as suicides than others; for example, an indigent or derelict person is more often judged a suicide than are other members of the community.

SUMMARY

It is clear that suicide is not a simple problem to study because, among other things, many difficulties obscure comprehension of the behavior. We know that suicide is a gradual process — it is not a "bolt from the blue" and it has forewarnings. We also know that suicide occurs more often in some situations than in others. People who are at risk for suicide give warnings that can be recognized by those close to them, both by changes in their behavior and by specific actions. Suicidal behavior is part of a continuum that moves in a logical pattern that is potentially understandable. Knowledge of the facts is critically important and may very well save lives.

REFERENCES

Asinof, E. *Craig and Joan*. New York: Viking, 1971.

Menninger, K.A. *Man Against Himself*. New York: Harcourt, Brace & World, 1938.

Pender, S.B. What are the current facts and fables about suicide? In D. Lester (ed.), *Suicide '93*. Denver: American Association of Suicidology, 1993.

Resnik, H.L.P Eroticized repetitive hangings. *American Journal of Psychotherapy* 26:4-21, 1972.

Shneidman, E.S., Farberow, N.L., and Leonard, C. *Some Facts about Suicide*. Washington, DC: U.S. Government Printing Office, 1965.

2

Problems in Suicide Research

In any research area, problems of design and interpretation must be solved before valid conclusions can be drawn. Some of these problems are general to all research, while others are unique to a particular topic. Problems exist because the natural world is a complex one and simple "facts" cannot be discovered at a glance. Information about any part of nature, and most particularly about behavior, must be obtained from very careful observation and analysis. If researchers do not work this way, they run the risk of seeing the world in the light of their own preconceptions rather than as it really is. In this chapter, some of the specific difficulties of investigating suicide will be discussed.

METHODOLOGICAL PROBLEMS IN SUICIDE RESEARCH

Defining the Behavior

In behavioral research, it is not infrequent for researchers to use a particular term or name to describe a phenomenon. When they try to compare their results with those of others, they find apparent contradictions because they have used the same label for different things or different labels for the same things.

Aware of this problem, suicidologists have deliberately mapped out strict criteria to define the behaviors of suicide. Neuringer (1962) pointed out that the greatest methodological problem in suicide research concerns the definition of the behavior. Neuringer's paper is one of the best attempts to analyze the different possible meanings for the term suicide, and this chapter makes repeated use of its ideas.

The first and most basic aspect of the definition of suicide concerns the actual behavior. Six categories of overt behavior can be noted: completed suicides, attempted suicides, suicide threats, thoughts of suicide, no preoccupation with suicide, and suicidal gestures, attempts that do not involve a real intent to die. People who make suicidal gestures include those reported by Kessel (1966) who calculated the lethal dose of a drug and then consumed half of that quantity. Some investigators such as Dorpat and Boswell (1963), have subdivided the attempted suicide category into gestures, ambivalent attempts and serious (potentially lethal) attempts. A group of European suicide researchers even suggested renaming attempted suicide "parasuicide" to get away from the notion that attempters are really trying to kill themselves (Kreitman et al., 1969). The term parasuicide is rarely used now, with many researchers in Europe commonly favoring the more specific expressions "self-injury," "self-poisoning" and "deliberate self-harm."

Canetto and Lester (1995) have objected to the use of the terms *attempted* and *completed* because they imply that attempters have somehow failed to finish the act, while completers have succeeded. They have suggested referring to these behaviors as "nonfatal" and "fatal" suicide, respectively.

Suicidal behavior can also be analyzed in terms of lethality — that is, the medical seriousness of the suicidal act. Information such as the number of pills taken or the height from which a jump is made allows us to calculate the chances that death will result.

The idea of lethality brings in a second basic dimension — the intent of a suicidal person. Even though a person may intend to die or survive, he may not always achieve his goal. Some people who complete suicide may have hoped that someone would save them, and attempters, who may really have wanted to die, were interrupted accidentally. Others may make mistakes in their attempts and not end up in the state they had hoped for. Thus, categorizing by intent may be more meaningful than categorizing by behavior.

Aaron Beck and his colleagues (1976) have proposed a scale of suicidal intent based on the objective circumstances of the suicidal act (such as whether the suicidal person isolated himself and whether he left a suicide note) and, in the case of attempters, on their answer to questions posed to them. This scale aroused great interest among researchers and has been used in a large number of studies.

Another important dimension of the definition of suicidal behavior concerns a person's degree of consciousness preceding the suicidal act. It has been claimed that certain individuals kill themselves while they are in an automatized state in which they are not aware of their actions (Long, 1959). However, as discussed in Chapter 16, there is no reliable evidence that these deaths are suicidal. This does not mean, however, that all forms of suicide are consciously planned. For example, according to Selzer and Payne (1962), people with an identified suicidal preoccupation had more automobile accidents than those without such a preoccupation. Schmidt and his co-workers (1976) claimed that 3 percent of single-crash fatalities were suicides. It may be true that the impulse toward suicide can be unconscious and that it may result in unplanned, "accidental" deaths.

Some suicidologists have considered long-term, gradual self-destructive behaviors as a form of suicide. Menninger (1938), for instance, used the term "chronic suicide" to refer to individuals who had histories of alcoholism, accident proneness, or other behaviors likely to result in premature death after a period of time.

Other investigators believe that a variety of self-destructive behaviors are suicidally motivated, if only in part, including chronic overeating, anorexia, self-mutilation, medication abuse and repeated risk-taking. Farberow (1980) has suggested calling these "indirect self-destructive behaviors." These behaviors have been found to be more common in certain groups such as the depressed elderly in nursing homes (Osgood et al., 1988-89).

The existence of these many possible categories of suicidal behavior is important for designing and interpreting research. As long as there is some suspicion that individuals in the different categories differ from one another, researchers must be sure that they know in which category a particular subject belongs. Only if they are fairly sure that two categories do not differ in terms of the factors concern with can researchers group them together. The necessity of conforming with this structure has led to many arguments among suicidologists about the difference between attempted and completed suicides. This special problem will be discussed below.

Methods of Investigation

Because researchers studying completed suicides obviously cannot get information from dead individuals, they must rely on two less satisfactory methods of investigation (Neuringer, 1962).

Residual Evidence

One way that investigators can obtain information about a person who commits suicide is to examine written material and other evidence that may have been left behind, such as suicide notes, diaries, letters and the results of previously obtained psychological test data. Another option is to gather residual information from the suicide's friends and relatives. Even though this method can be useful, for several reasons, it is less than perfect. One problem is that observational distortion may occur; in other words, friends and relatives may not know or even remember what the person was really like and their memories may be colored by the fact that the person committed suicide. Also, the validity of the information they give can be difficult to determine. This is true not only of reminiscences about the suicide, but also about material he may have written. If, for example, his diary mentions a tragic secret love affair, there may be no way to know whether the relationship really existed or if it was only a fantasy. Either possible scenario could provide vital information about the suicide, but because each is important in a very different way, it is critical to know whether a given event actually occurred.

Several researchers have devised structured methods for interviewing the friends and relatives of people who committed suicide so that information may be obtained in a standardized format (Maris, 1981). These "psychological autopsies," as they are called, have provided important insights into an individual's suicidal process.

Another problem with using residual evidence is the proper establishment of control groups. What, for example, should suicide notes be compared with? There are a number of possibilities: suicide notes written by nonsuicidal subjects who pretend, at the request of the researcher, that they are about to kill themselves; letters of nonsuicidal content written by suicidal people; or letters of nonsuicidal content written by nonsuicidal people. While none of these possibilities offers an ideal control group, each has its own set of advantages and disadvantages.

Substitute Subjects

A researcher can assemble a group of living subjects that he feels are representative of completed suicides prior to their deaths. Usually these substitute subjects are people who have attempted suicide. However, Neuringer (1962) argued that because suicide attempters do not resemble suicide completers closely enough, this method is not reliable. How do we determine whether using substitute subjects is a valid method of investigation? The issue is actually an empirical one, because it should be possible to determine what differences exist between completers and attempters, thereby enabling researchers to create a valid group of substitute subjects.

To demonstrate the difficulty of using substitute subjects in this type of suicide research, Farberow and Shneidman (1955) compared threatened, attempted and completed suicides and found no differences in demographic variables, socioeconomic variables or early family environment. However, these groups did differ in psychiatric diagnosis, method of attempting suicide and previous suicidal history.

In their 1963 study, Dorpat and Boswell (1963) found that the ratio of men to women changed monotonically from suicide gestures to completed suicide. This would suggest that it is valid to extrapolate, not only from attempted to completed suicides, but even from gestures to completed suicides.

Based on the above findings, Lester's team (1975, 1979) argued that much can be learned about completed suicides from a study of attempted suicides *only if* they are classified into groups that are based on suicidal intent. They then classified a sample of attempted suicides based on their intent to die (based both from self-reports and objective circumstances surrounding the suicidal act) and found that depression scores and hopelessness scores increased monotonically as suicidal intent increased. They argued that these monotonic trends could be extended to make predictions about completed suicides, the group with the highest suicidal intent.

A Continuum of Suicidal Behavior

Having said all of the above, it may be that dividing the behavior of suicide into attempters and completers is an mistake, a gross simplification. It is important to remember that all suicidal acts occur along a continuum that ranges from highly lethal to noninjurious and to describe an act as an attempted suicide or as a completed suicide simply is only emphasizing the two endmost points on the continuum.

Special Problems of Control

As noted above, it is hard to assemble a proper comparison group for completed suicides. Unfortunately, the same problem occurs when attempted suicides are the object of study. Even experimenter control of the information about the attempters is sometimes hard to achieve. Several factors can contribute to this difficulty.

Feedback Effects from the Attempt

Often, when research is conducted on suicide attempters, information is collected immediately after the attempt. This introduces many confounding variables. After attempting suicide, people are not necessarily the same as they were before it. There may be a cathartic effect from the attempt (Van Praag and Plutchik, 1985); in other words, the individual's anger or misery may be temporarily

assuaged as a result of the attempt. The information that they give
to an interviewer about their feelings may not be the same as it
would have been before the attempt. Therapeutic intervention, even
if it is confined to stomach pumping, may change the attempter's
feelings in one direction or another. The ways in which other people have reacted to the attempt (such as scorn, horror or sympathy)
may influence the attempter. Also, attempters may have brain or
other tissue damage as a result of the attempt. Finally, they may try
to act as "normal" as possible in order to facilitate their release from
the hospital. Ideally, data from before as well as after the suicide
attempt should be used, but such data are very difficult to collect
because suicide is relatively uncommon.

Effects of Hospitalization

In many situations, hospitalized suicide attempters are treated differently than other patients. They may be guarded closely and sus-
piciously. If they attempted to commit suicide again while in the
hospital, this could cause guilt, anxiety or even hostility in the staff.
As a result the suicidal patient may feel guilty or rejected, even
though such feelings were not present before the attempt.

Adequate Control Populations

Ideally, control groups in research on suicide should be nonsuicidal.
In practice, totally nonsuicidal subjects are difficult to obtain. Even
if people profess to be without any suicidal tendencies, the
researcher must remember that many people may be reluctant to
confess to having suicidal behavior and ideation. At one time or
another, most people have at least thought about committing suicide. Even though it is hard to select an adequate control group, it is
possible. As noted above, suicidal involvement is not an all-or-noth-
ing matter. It is certainly possible to select a control group of people
who are less seriously suicidal than the group they are being compared to. As long as the researcher uses two groups that do not
overlap on the continuum of suicidal involvement, meaningful
research can be conducted.

Other Methodological Problems

The subjects in any control group should be matched on all relevant
variables with the other comparison group. However, the range of
relevant variables is so enormous that such a task is practically
impossible, especially because suicide is a relatively rare behavior

and subjects are scarce. This requirement, therefore, poses a real problem for suicide research. Sometimes researchers match their groups for age, sex and psychiatric disorder and the matching is rarely, if ever, more complete than that. Therefore if differences between suicidal and nonsuicidal groups are found they may be caused by the variables on which the subjects are unmatched. For example, if the control group and a group of completed suicides were not matched for marital status, some factor like the number of children might appear to differentiate them, since the completed suicides would be less likely to be married, and thus less likely to have children.

In addition, the particular subject population that is chosen may bias the results. Slewers and Davidoff (1943) compared two groups of attempted suicides: those admitted to a general hospital and those admitted to a psychiatric hospital. The two groups differed on many variables. Those in the general hospital were younger and less disturbed than those in the psychiatric hospital. They also differed in occupation, religious affiliation, method of suicide used and the presence of organic disease.

Not only are different groups of suicides unlike each other on important variables, but samples of suicides may not be representative of the total suicidal population. When Shneidman and Farberow (1961) traced 5,906 attempted suicides in Los Angeles County, they could find sufficient data on only 2,652. Also, research in other areas has shown that untraced persons may differ significantly from those who are traced (Lester, 1969). The same objection applies to studies of suicide notes. Shneidman and Farberow reported that 36 percent of completed suicides and 1 percent of attempted suicides left notes that were found. To what extent are the note writers typical of suicidal people in general?

Finally, we should consider the problem of level of statistical significance for research on suicide. It has been difficult to find many significant differences between suicidal and nonsuicidal subjects. Neuringer and Kolstoe (1966) suggested that a less stringent level for deciding that a result is statistically significant should be accepted for suicide research, because many important relationships might otherwise be missed. However, changing the required significance level would mean that many unreliable and false relationships would be accepted. It is hard enough for results to be replicated at the present probability levels. We could make a case for demanding more stringent significance levels so that the results of suicide research would be reliable. If no reliable results were then to be found, it would be clear that thinking about the causes of suicide requires a drastic reconceptualization rather than just a change in significance levels.

SUMMARY

Research on suicide almost always involves correlational rather than experimental methods. For this reason, it may be difficult to accurately determine in which direction causality is operating, because correlational studies do not permit inferences about cause and effect to be drawn. For example, if unemployment is found to be correlated with suicidal behavior, it may be that unemployment causes suicidal behavior, that suicidal behavior causes unemployment, or that some third variable (such as psychiatric disorder) causes both unemployment and suicidal behavior. Choosing a sample and establishing control groups also cause problems for suicide research, as does deciding whether attempters and completers should be considered as different groups. Biased results may be found when research is done on a particular sample that is not typical of all suicidal people.

REFERENCES

Beck, A.T., Weissman, A., Lester, D. and Trexler, L. Classification of suicidal behaviors. *Archives of General Psychiatry* 33:835-837, 1976.

Canetto, S.S. and Lester, D. (eds.) *Suicidal Behavior in Women*. New York: Springer, 1995.

Dorpat, T.L. and Boswell, J.W. An evaluation of suicidal intent in suicide attempts. *Comprehensive Psychiatry* 4:117-125, 1963.

Farberow, N.L. *The Many Faces of Suicide*. New York: McGraw-Hill, 1980.

Farberow, N.L. and Shneidman, E.S. Attempted, threatened, and completed suicide. *Journal of Abnormal and Social Psychology* 50:230,1995.

Kessel, N. The respectability of self-poisoning and the fashion of survival. *Journal of Psychosomatic Research* 10:29-36, 1996.

Kreitman, N., Philip, A.E., Greer, S. and Bagley, C. Parasuicide. *British Journal of Psychiatry* 115:747-748, 1969.

Lester, D. The subject as a source of bias in psychological research. *Journal of General Psychology* 81:237-248, 1969.

Lester, D., Beck, A.T. and Trexler, L. Extrapolation from attempted suicide to completed suicide. *Journal of Abnormal Psychology* 84:563-566, 1975.

Lester, D., Beck, A.T. and Mitchell, B. Extrapolation from attempted suicide to completed suicide. *Journal of Abnormal Psychology* 88:78-80, 1979.

Long, R.H. Barbiturates, automatization, and suicide. *Insurance Counseling Journal*, April, 1959, pp. 299-307.

Maris, R.W. *Pathways to Suicide*. Baltimore: Johns Hopkins University Press, 1981.

Menninger, K. *Man Against Himself*. New York: Harcourt, Brace and World, 1938.

Neuringer, C. and Kolstoe, R.H. Suicide research and the non-rejection of the null hypothesis. *Perceptual and Motor Skills* 22:115-118, 1966.

Neuringer, C. Methodological problems in suicide research. *Journal of Consulting Psychology* 26:273-278, 1962.

Osgood, N.J., Brant, B.A. and Lipman, A.A. Patterns of suicidal behavior in long-term care facilities. *Omega* 19:69-78, 1988-89.

Schmidt, C.W., Shaffer, J.W., Banks, W., et al. Suicide by vehicular crash. In V. Aalberg (ed.), *Proceedings of the 9th International Congress for Suicide Prevention*. Helsinki: Finnish Association for Mental Health, 1978.

Selzer, M.L. and Payne, C.E. Automobile accidents, suicide, and unconscious motivation. *American Journal of Psychiatry* 119:237-240, 1962.

Shneidman, E.S. and Farberow, N.L. Statistical comparisons between committed and attempted suicides. In N.L. Farberow and E.S. Shneidman (eds.) *The Cry for Help*. New York: McGraw-Hill, 1961.

Siewers, A.B. and Davidoff, E. Attempted suicide. *Psychiatric Quarterly* 17:520-534, 1943.

Van Praag, H. and Plutchik, R. An empirical study of the cathartic effect of attempted suicide. *Psychiatry Research* 16:123-130, 1985.

3

Labeling Death:
Taxonomies of Dying

For centuries people have believed that there is a definite moment when the transition from life to death occurs. Long ago, people attempted to pinpoint the moment of transition by weighing a dying person on a scale in an attempt to determine when the soul leaves the body. They thought that a person's weight would decrease slightly as the soul departed the body.

Advances in medicine have raised legitimate questions about exactly when death occurs. For example, 100 years ago, a person whose heart had stopped beating and who had stopped breathing was considered dead; today, we know that a person in the same circumstance can sometimes be revived. This has led us to reexamine not only our understanding of physical death and when it occurs, but also our understanding of psychological death and when it occurs.

THE PSYCHOLOGICAL MOMENT OF DEATH

When the goal is to cure physical illness, bodily signs of death are objective evidence that can be used. In the study of suicide, an equally important consideration is the subjective judgment of the conditions under which a person is considered dead. The question of the psychological moment of death is an interesting one in itself, because not all people agree on the answer. This question is also important to the study of suicide, because self-destruction would be more likely if a person were considered subjectively "dead" even though he was objectively still living and conscious.

In one study of the subjective time of death (Kalish, 1965), college students were asked to choose one of seven alternatives as the circumstances under which a person is considered to be dead. The choices were: (1) when he first learns he is going to die; (2) when he first enters a hospital, knowing that he will never leave alive; (3) when he first enters a nursing home, knowing that he will never leave alive; (4) when he loses self-awareness; (5) when he becomes very senile; (6) when he wants to die or gives up on life; and (7) when his heart stops beating.

Only half of the students used the biological criterion of cessation of heartbeats as the event that signified death. The others used psychosocial criteria instead: 35 percent said the person was dead when he lost self-awareness, and 35 percent said wanting to die or giving up on life indicated death. (Some students checked more than one alternative, so the figures total more than 100 percent.)

There seem to be four basic criteria for defining death (Kalish, 1966):

1. *Physical death:*

    a. *Biological death*: when the organs stop functioning.

    b. *Clinical death:* when the organism no longer functions but the organs continue to live. If a person fatally injured in an accident is kept alive mechanically until his heart can be transplanted, he is clinically dead for some time before his biological death.

2. *Psychological death:* The individual ceases to be aware of his own existence. He does not know who he is or even that he is. This can occur, of course, well before physical death if the person is in a coma.

3. *Social death:*

    a. *Self-perceived:* the individual accepts the notion that he is, for all practical purposes, dead. An example of this would occur in the case of "voodoo death" (Lester, 1972). The person believes that a spell or curse has been placed on him and that he will die within some brief period. He stops functioning, refuses nourishment and waits for death to occur, which it often does.

    b. *Other-perceived:* people who know the individual behave as if he is dead or nonexistent. An elderly relative is placed in a nursing home and forgotten. In ancient times, lepers were cast out of society and expected never to have social contact with healthy people.

4. *Anthropological death:* The individual is cut off from a particular community and referred to as if he is dead. An Orthodox

Jewish family, for example, may mourn for a child who marries a Gentile as if he had physically died. (When he dies biologically, however, they may mourn again, thus showing that they discriminate between anthropological and physical death.)

CLASSIFYING DEATH STATES

The established medical scheme for classifying states of death stresses the causes and the modes of death. Four modes are commonly recognized: accidental death, homicide, suicide and natural death. This classification is adequate for its original purpose — the ascription of responsibility for death to the right source or cause. However, it does not allow fine enough distinctions for use when a person has been motivated to seek his own death. For example, when a person deliberately provokes another person to murder him, the death will be classified as a homicide, but this categorization does not take into account the victim's suicidal motivation.

Shneidman (1963) has proposed an alternative classification that allows a more meaningful description of death. First, the system involves a new classification of the behaviors associated with death:

1. *Cessation* is defined as the stopping of any (further) conscious experience. It is the demise of psychic processes.

2. *Termination* is the end of the body's physiological functioning. In the Christian view of an afterlife, termination can occur without cessation.

3. *Interruption* is the temporary stopping of conscious awareness, as in coma.

4. *Continuation* is the ongoing conscious experience of events.

These four terms define physical death as it is experienced by the dying person and by those caring for him. A second variable in Shneidman's classification involves the role of the deceased in his own death. The following four basic roles were proposed:

1. *Intentioned (or premeditated).* The person plays a direct and conscious role in his own demise. Many, but not all, suicidal deaths could be labeled "intentioned," as could some homicidal deaths, like the victim-precipitated homicides mentioned earlier (Wolfgang, 1959). Some deaths that are considered accidental might be intentioned, as when a person teases an animal until it kills him. A natural death can sometimes be inten-

tioned too, as when a person deliberately exposes himself to disease. Clearly, all intentioned deaths are suicidal, but their suicidal aspects may not be noted by those who determine the mode of death. Some deaths may occur because of a person's own deliberate actions and yet not be intentioned.

2. *Subintentioned (or submeditated)*. The person plays an indirect, covert or unconscious role in his demise, such as when he fails to act for his own best welfare. Some suicidal deaths could be subintentioned; for example, a diabetic might go on a drinking binge, knowing that the alcohol is killing him.

3. *Unintentioned (or unmeditated)*. The person plays no significant role in his own demise.

4. *Contraintentioned*. When the person acts as if he is about to die or threatens to commit suicide, but has no intention of doing so, he is playing a contraintended role.

Because Shneidman's classification was never widely used, we will use the ordinary terminology in this book. Nevertheless, the reader will benefit from understanding the kind of analysis of death implied in Shneidman's taxonomy as he reads more about suicidal behavior.

THE CLASSIFICATION OF SUICIDAL BEHAVIOR

For the most part, suicidal acts are classified in terms of their outcome. For example, if a person deliberately tries to kill himself, but does not die, he is said to have *attempted* suicide. If he does die as a result of this act, he is said to have committed suicide. I agree with the term attempted suicide and shall use it, but, instead of using the term committed suicide for those who die, I prefer *completed*, a term that is now more widely used. The idea that a person can complete suicide stresses that suicidal behaviors are ranged on a continuum from mildly lethal to completely lethal.

Classifying suicidal acts into suicide attempters and completers is useful, but it may obscure facts about the motivation of the suicidal behavior; for example a person who fully intends to die is rescued before he can complete the act or a person who only wants to make a dramatic gesture accidentally dies because the intervention he expected doesn't occur.

If the nature of suicidal behavior is obscured by the attempted versus completed dichotomy, why is it still used? One reason is a longstanding belief among suicidologists that those who attempt and those who complete suicide are very different kinds of people. For example, as I will discuss in Chapter 12, more males complete suicide and more females attempt it. However, there is little information available to help us determine whether or not the populations of attempters and completers are really different. Nonetheless, to allow for the possibility that the groups vary in quality rather than simply in severity of suicidal impulses, I will not group attempters and completers together when discussing suicide research.

DEATH BY ACCIDENT

According to Shneidman's classification, a person may bring about his own death because of a "subintentioned" wish — a wish of which one is not fully aware. This raises the question of whether some people who die in car accidents (especially in single-car-crash fatalities) resemble those whose death is intentioned and brought about by other means. (It may even be the case that an automobile is used as a means of premeditated suicide.)

It has been suggested that people who have a history of accidents while they are driving also have a history of suicidal preoccupation (Selzer and Payne, 1962; Selzer et al., 1968). However, Isherwood's group (1982) found that people who attempted suicide had also experienced more recent stressors of all kinds than people who had been in car crashes. The suicide attempters were also more depressed and neurotic, and exhibited little participation in sports. Furthermore, Jenkins and Sainsbury (1980) found that the distributions of the deceased by age and by the month in which death occurred were very different for those who were killed in single car crashes and those who completed suicide. Thus the resemblance of suicides to single-car-crash victims in general seems minimal, though a small proportion of single-car-crash victims may indeed be suicides.

OTHER SELF-DESTRUCTIVE BEHAVIORS

Many forms of behavior are not immediately lethal but lead, in the long run, to self-injury or death. Some writers, such as Menninger (1938), have considered these behaviors to be closely related to suicide. Conditions such as alcoholism, drug addiction and polysurgery (the practice of having multiple operations for no real medical reason) may all be considered as subintentioned suicidal behavior. Some of them are quite effective as "interruptions," since they can produce temporary unconsciousness. Mild self-injurious behaviors such as wrist-slashing, nail-biting and hair-pulling may also be related to suicide. Menninger was willing to accept some of these behaviors as qualitatively similar to suicide. Because no real research on this question has been done, it remains a matter of opinion.

OFFICIAL STATISTICS ON SUICIDE

When a coroner decides whether a death is a suicide, or when a county health board issues statistics about the suicide rate in its area, fine points such as whether nail-biting resembles suicide are not considered. In fact, one may wonder exactly what they do consider. One suicidologist, Douglas (1967), has severely criticized the accuracy of certification of suicidal deaths. Douglas pointed out that the meaning of the term "suicide" may vary tremendously over time, among geographical regions and among different religious groups. For example, there are reports of a coroner in the United States who would only certify a death as suicide if a suicide note was found with the body. Because it is estimated that only 10 to 40 percent of people who kill themselves leave notes, it seems likely that this particular coroner was grossly underestimating the number of suicides in his area.

Not only is it possible that there is a systematic bias about the certification of deaths by suicide, but there may also be deliberate attempts to conceal suicidal deaths. There are clearly many reasons to attempt to hide the fact that a death was caused by suicide. Some religious groups refuse normal funeral rites to people who commit suicide. Insurance policies often do not pay the survivors any benefits beyond the premiums after a death by suicide within two years of taking out the policy, and they frequently pay more for a death judged to be accidental than for a suicide or a natural death. We can only presume that the reporting of suicidal deaths would be more accurate if less opprobrium were attached to suicide by society.

Until better criteria are available for deciding when a suicide has occurred, coroners can hardly be expected to use consistent decision methods. Essentially, each coroner now determines himself whether particular tests should be made (e.g., for the presence of barbiturates in the body). Coroners also set their own standards for inferring whether the dead person was motivated toward suicide. These standards are personally and culturally determined; for example, a woman who was known to have been disappointed in love might be certified as a suicide when a man would not.

Many studies have documented the underreporting of suicide. Clarke-Finnegan and Fahy (1983) examined the records in the coroner's office for Galway County, Ireland, and found that the actual suicide rate was probably more than twice as high as the officially reported rate (13.1 per 100,000 per year as opposed to 5.8).

Some attempts are being made to find good criteria for deciding when a person has been motivated toward suicide. At the Los Angeles Suicide Prevention Center, for example, psychologists and psychiatrists have participated regularly in "psychological autopsies." In these investigations, predeath activities are studied. The family, friends and physician of the deceased are interviewed, and an attempt is made to develop an accurate picture of the last days of the person's life. However, because the psychological autopsy requires hours of work by many trained personnel, one wonders how many coroners actually use this method to help them certify deaths accurately.

SUMMARY

Death is a gradual process, and no one moment can be identified as the time when it occurs. From the viewpoint of suicidology, the question of when physical death occurs is less important than the individual's subjective experience and understanding of death. He may consider himself "as good as dead" when his body is still functioning, or he may expect his consciousness and awareness to continue beyond bodily death. Another important question involves the role the person plays in his own death. For example, he may help bring his death about without being conscious of doing so. Official certifications of death do not usually attend to any of these subtle questions, and they probably serve to underestimate the actual incidence of suicide.

REFERENCES

Clarke-Finnegan, M. and Fahy, T. Suicide rates in Ireland. *Psychological Medicine* 13:385-391,1983.

Douglas, J.D. *The Social Meanings of Suicide*. Princeton, NJ: Princeton University Press, 1967.

Isherwood, J., Adams, K.S. and Hornblow, A. Life event stress, psychosocial factors, suicide attempts and auto-accident proclivity. *Journal of Psychosomatic Research* 26:371-383, 1982.

Jenkins, J. and Sainsbury, P. Single-car road deaths. *British Medical Journal* 281:1041, 1980.

Kalish, R.A. A continuum of subjectively perceived death. Paper given at meeting of the Gerontological Society, Los Angeles, 1965.

Kalish, R.A. Life and death. Paper given at meeting of the American

Psychological Association, New York, 1966.

Lester, D. Voodoo death. *American Anthropologist* 74:386-390, 1972.

Menninger, K. *Man Against Himself.* New York: Harcourt, Brace & World, 1938.

Selzer, M.L. and Payne, C.E. Automobile accidents, suicide, and unconscious motivation. *American Journal of Psychiatry* 119:237-240, 1962.

Selzer, M.L., Rogers, J.E. and Kern, S. Fatal accidents. *American Journal of Psychiatry* 124:1028-1036, 1968.

Shneidman, E.S. Orientations toward death. In R. White (ed.) *The Study of Lives.* New York: Atherton, 1963.

Wolfgang, M.E. Suicide by means of victim-precipitated homicide. *Journal of Clinical and Experimental Psychopathology* 20:335-349, 1959.

4

Heredity, Environment and Suicide

When more than one person in a family has killed himself, gossip may begin to circulate about a hereditary taint in the family that will inevitably cause more suicides. The possibility of the inheritance of a suicidal tendency may create anxiety in the living members of the family. Even a child who is too young to remember his father's suicide may wonder whether the same death is in store for him, whether he has something to do with causing this death or not.

Is there a real basis for people's suspicions and fears? Can a predisposition to suicide be passed along genetically in the same way as eye color or hemophilia? Or, alternatively, is suicide purely the result of an individual's experiences? This chapter will attempt to address these questions using the research findings that are currently available.

GENETIC FACTORS

The question of whether human traits are inherited or determined by the environment is always difficult to address. For example, it can be argued that if the results of genetic factors do not manifest until later in life, they cannot be reliably identified as such, since, by that time, the environment has already exerted a strong influence on the individual. There is evidence that even the environment of the uterus in the period between conception and birth can influence behavior. Nevertheless, some attempts have been made to try to trace genetic factors in suicide (Lester, 1986).

Some years ago, a common approach to this problem was to study family trees. This method does not differentiate hereditary from environmental influences, since no two people ever experience exactly the same family environment. (In a family of four children, for example, the eldest will experience an environment that in her case contains two younger brothers and a very young sister, while the youngest will experience two older brothers and a very superior elder sister.) Nevertheless, the study of genealogical tables indicates that some families have a very high incidence of suicide, which appears to confirm the belief that suicide does not "strike" at random.

One famous example of a family whose members exhibited suicidal behavior in many generations is that of the Hemingways (Lester, 1987). Ernest Hall was born in 1840 in Britain, emigrated to America, fought in the Civil War and then moved to Chicago where he worked in the cutlery trade. In 1905, dying and in great pain, he planned to shoot himself. Learning of this, his son-in-law removed the bullets from his pistol, and when Ernest Hall made the attempt to kill himself, he fired an empty gun.

In 1928, this son-in-law, Ed Hemingway, a doctor, was suffering from diabetes that he had failed to diagnose and treat. That year he had also suffered financial losses from land speculation in Florida. He came home from lunch one day and shot himself with a .32 caliber Smith and Wesson revolver. Ed Hemingway was found by his 13 year-old son, Leicester, who had stayed home from school because he had the flu.

Ed Hemingway had six children, three of whom committed suicide. His famous son, Ernest Hemingway, shot and killed himself in 1961. He had been suffering from a severe depression and the effects of several physical ailments, mostly stemming from his chronic alcohol abuse. A daughter, Ursula Hemingway Jepson, diagnosed with terminal cancer, killed herself with an overdose of morphine in 1966. Leicester Hemingway, suffering from diabetes that had required the amputation of his legs, killed himself in 1982. More recently, actress and model Margaux Hemingway, the great novelist's granddaughter, died from a large overdose of antidepressants in 1996.

It appears on the surface that suicidal behavior may have been genetically passed from generation to generation in the Hemingway family. However, what is more likely is that a predisposition to depressive illness, rather than a suicidal tendency, may have been passed on, and that the members of this family learned a suicidal pattern of behavior. The Hemingways seemed to have decided that, when faced with suffering, suicide is an acceptable method of escape.

A more appropriate way to study genetic factors in suicide involves research with twins. Monozygotic twins, who develop from a single ovum, are genetically identical. Dizygotic twins, who start their development as separate ova, are no more similar genetically than nontwin siblings. In a classic study, Kallman (1953) followed 18 pairs of identical twins and 21 pairs of fraternal twins among whom at least one of the twins had killed himself. If suicide was genetically caused, one would expect the identical twin pairs to have concordant behavior; that is, if one twin committed suicide, his co-twin would also exhibit suicidal behavior. Among fraternal twin pairs, concordance would be no higher than among ordinary siblings. Kallman did not find any difference between concordance of suicide in monozygotic and in dizygotic twin pairs.

A recent review of Kallman's and other twin studies (Lester, 1986) found evidence that monozygotic twins do have a higher concordance for suicide than dizygotic twins, but that no study had examined the concordance for suicide in monozygotic twins who had been separated at birth (or early in life) and had been reared apart. This situation would eliminate the possibility that identical twins may be treated very differently from fraternal twins, and that similarity in child rearing could account for their greater similarity in the target behavior being studied. This requirement has been met in studies of the inheritance of psychiatric illness and such personality traits as intelligence, but not as yet for suicidal behavior.

CONSTITUTIONAL FACTORS

To some extent, a person's physical constitution is influenced by genetic factors and to some extent it is determined by his environment (as in the case of childhood diet). Many investigators have examined physiological differences between suicidal and nonsuicidal subjects. Although genetic factors do not seem to be operative in suicide, perhaps the combination of certain hereditary and environmental effects is instrumental in leading to suicide. Investigation of this problem has stressed three main areas: physical state (illness versus good health), physique and physiological (biochemical) state.

Physical State

Illness can produce stress that may contribute to the development of suicidal behavior. A number of studies have found that the physical health of suicides a few months before their death was worse than that of a nonsuicidal group. In one study (Dorpat et al., 1968), 70 percent of the completed suicides appeared to have had an acute illness at the time of death. The illness seemed to have contributed to suicide by affecting mood. Depressive reactions were produced by fear of death, pain and surgery and through the social isolation that accompanies illness. More recently, Hjortso (1987) found that 30 percent of male and 27 percent of female completed suicides had known illnesses, and when they included illnesses that were suspected, these percentages increased to 42 percent and 31 percent, respectively.

It must be noted that some researchers have found no relation between suicidal behavior and physical illness in their studies. For example, Barraclough and Hughes (1987) found no excess of illness or handicaps in a sample of completed suicides as compared to living controls. No one, however, has reported a negative relationship (i.e., an association between suicide with good health and nonsuicide and poor health). A recent review of the research (Lester, 1992) concluded that suicide rates were higher than normal in those suffering from AIDS, limb amputation, epilepsy, Huntington's disease and spinal cord injuries, and those on dialysis.

Poor health can probably contribute to suicidal behavior, but it is one of the less important factors in actually causing suicide.

Physique

A relationship between physique and personality exists in many implicit notions of personality, such as "the jolly fat man" and the dangerous man with "a lean and hungry look." Sheldon (1942) proposed that human beings could be assigned to one of three predominant body types, each of which was associated with particular personality traits. Fat people with highly developed viscera were given the name "endomorphs" and were thought to be sociable and pleasure-loving. "Mesomorphs" were heavily muscled and were thought to be rather brash and insensitive. "Ectomorphs" were thin and had little muscular development; they were considered shy, intellectual and hypersensitive to all kinds of stimulation. Sheldon believed that endomorphs had a strong aversion to death and that suicide was rare among them. Ectomorphs, on the other hand, with their shyness and hypersensitivity, were thought to have frequent suicidal tendencies.

Some studies have examined the possible relationship between a person's weight and suicide. In general, it appears that underweight or overweight people are more likely to kill themselves than people of normal weight. For example, in their study, Thomas and Greenstreet (1973) followed medical students and found that those who eventually completed suicide were more often underweight and ectomorphic when they were at medical school than the other medical students in their subject group.

We must remember, when thinking about physique and suicide, that causality need not work only in one direction. People who become suicidal may have changes in physique due to their mood. They may change their dietary habits and become overweight or underweight because of their obsession with suicide.

Physiological State

The research that has been done on biochemical changes and suicide is far too complex to be dealt with here in detail. However, a great deal of research has been conducted in recent years on the levels of several different neurotransmitters in the brain in people suffering from major psychiatric illnesses and also in people who attempt and complete suicide. This research has studied the levels of the neurotransmitters and the density of neurotransmitter receptor sites in the brain, as well as the levels of the breakdown products of these neurotransmitters in cerebrospinal fluid and urine. A review of this research (Lester, 1988) indicates that people suffering from severe depressions most likely have a deficit in the level of serotonin in the brain, and among those who are suicidal, these levels seem to be especially low. Recently, Lester (1995) reviewed the research on the levels of 5-hydroxyindoleacetic acid (the breakdown product of serotonin) in the cerebrospinal fluid and concluded that the role of serotonin in suicidal behavior had been demonstrated convincingly.

It is likely that future research will pinpoint the biochemical abnormalities in suicidal individuals more precisely, perhaps even devising a biochemical test to predict severe depression and suicidal behavior.

THE EFFECT OF THE ENVIRONMENT

What is the effect of environment on suicidal behavior? Is it possible that learning and experience in the course of life are determining factors? Our major emphasis in this discussion will be on comparisons of suicidal behavior in different cultural groups. The problem of the influence of individual experiences on suicidal behavior, which is also relevant to this issue, will be discussed at length in the next chapter.

It is clear that there are considerable differences in incidence of suicidal behavior from one culture to another. In most cases, quite a lot is known about the culture under consideration, including its child-rearing practices, its values and its social organization. Cross-cultural comparisons have thus presented a very valuable means of testing hypotheses about the causes of suicidal behavior.

Suicide occurs in primitive, nonliterate societies as well as in modern ones, and ethnographers have collected a considerable amount of information on suicidal behavior in primitive societies. This discussion, however, will be limited to investigation of cross-comparisons between well-documented modern social groups. This limitation will be imposed despite the fact that primitive suicidal behavior is often very interesting, because much of the information collected by early ethnographers is not especially reliable. After Naroll (1962) analyzed the reports of early ethnographers in an attempt to find sources of bias, he concluded that estimates of suicidal behavior are biased by the inaccuracy of the informants and by the narrowness of the ethnographers' data. When modern developed societies are studied, it is possible to obtain data from so many sources that existing biases will cancel each other out. It is also possible to go back and remeasure suspicious data, which cannot easily be done in the case of a specific ethnographic field study.

Cultural Differences in Reacting to Crises

Because suicidal behavior appears to occur most often in a crisis situation, it is worthwhile to note that reactions to crisis are strongly determined by culture. One culture may condone reactions that are highly emotional and even criticize a person who remains calm, while another may insist on complete stoicism in the face of crisis. Some of the crisis-related behaviors described in this section may be conceptualized as possible examples of subintentioned suicide, which was discussed in the previous chapter.

Trautman (1961) noted that Puerto Rican women in a crisis situation may respond by the hysterical *ataque nerviosa*, in which the individual withdraws from the problem by falling to the ground in a stupor. McCandless (1968) has looked at the differences between people of Indian and of African origin who live in Guyana. The Indians have little in the way of culturally sanctioned behavior for displaying rage; they are simply supposed to obey their laws by holding back their feelings toward others no matter what the crisis. In contrast, the Africans in Guyana have many culturally approved ways of expressing their feelings to others during a crisis. It is understandable that the suicide rate is very low among the African population and high among the Indians. Another way of responding to a crisis is seen in the frenzied state known by the Malay term *amok*, which differs dramatically from most culturally approved Western responses to crisis situations. The person who runs amok essentially does everything he has been told not to do. He is highly destructive to property and to people who get in his way. Above all, however, he "tempts fate" by calling out special words that are forbidden to be spoken — such as the magic name for tigers, which is thought to attract them to the scene. If the words really had the power attributed to them by the culture, his behavior would, in effect, be suicidal.

The reader may notice that, although amok is very different from any crisis response presently approved by Western cultures, it is somewhat similar to behaviors such as heavy and belligerent drinking or reckless driving during a crisis. Looking at the historical background of modern Western societies, we find that the Vikings had a culturally sanctioned state known as being "berserk," in which a warrior hurled himself into combat with animals or other men without thought for his own safety. Fortunately for the "berserker," other warriors were frightened by this behavior and tended to flee rather than taking advantage of the berserker's poorly guarded approach.

Cultural Differences in Suicidal Behavior

There has been a great deal of research on suicidal behavior in different cultures. In a study of the various cultural groups living in Hawaii, Richard Kalish (1968) determined that the ratio of completed suicides to suicide attempts ranged from 5:100 for Hawaiian Puerto Ricans to 73:100 for Hawaiian Chinese. Among the native Hawaiians, Filipinos and Puerto Ricans, there was a higher percentage of young people who completed suicide, while among the Koreans, Japanese and Chinese, there was a higher percentage of older people who completed suicide.

Suicidal behavior in Japan differs considerably from that in the United States (Iga, 1986). Many more women commit suicide in Japan than in the United States. The Japanese suicide rate is higher in rural than in urban areas, which is also the opposite of the American pattern. In Japan, the age group with the highest suicide rate is 75 and older (Lester and Tallmer, 1994), whereas in the United States, there are two age groups with the highest rates: first, those aged 75 and older and second, those aged 25 to 34. Iga attributed these differences in suicidal behavior to a deficiency in personality development (i.e., psychological immaturity), a strong sense of shame after failure and a more favorable attitude toward suicide among the Japanese. However, there seems to be no significant evidence for any differences between Americans and Japanese in terms of maturity of personality. However, suicide has long been socially accepted in Japan as a solution to serious personal problems. In the days of the Japanese Empire, the ceremony of *seppuku* was considered to be an appropriate way for a respectable person to negate a humiliation that had come upon him. Perhaps this traditional approval of suicide under certain prescribed conditions accounts for the higher rural suicide rate in Japan, in that the old customs are more likely to persist in rural areas.

Suicide in Scandinavia

Many suicidologists have tried to explain the peculiar differences in suicide rates that existed in Scandinavia in the 1970s and 1980s. In 1970, the completed suicide rate was almost three times as high (about 22 per 100,000) in both Sweden and Denmark as it was in Norway, where the rate was only about 8 per 100,000 per year. (By 1990, however, these suicide rates had changed to 17, 24, and 15 per 100,000 per year, respectively.)

One hypothesis about the differences that existed in the 1960s and 1970s, frequently voiced by political conservatives of the time, was that the establishment of a welfare state led to a high suicide rate. Their explanation was that a welfare system reduces the general incentive to work, promotes boredom, diminishes the zest for living, creates a lack of tolerance for frustration and thus engenders a desire among the population to commit suicide. In 1965, Farber attempted to determine whether the welfare state actually did affect the suicide rate. He stated that the differences between the suicide rates in Norway and Denmark exist in spite of the fact that both have welfare systems. When the welfare system was instituted in Denmark, the suicide rate actually showed a moderate decline, especially among the older people who benefitted most from the welfare system. Farber also noted that Saskatchewan had the most highly developed welfare system in Canada, but that its suicide rate was lower than that of the neighboring provinces that did not have such a system. Similarly, in the United States, the suicide rate decreased after the social programs of the New Deal were introduced.

In 1965, Hendin made a psychoanalytic attempt to explain the differences among the suicide rates of Norway, Denmark and Sweden. To gain an understanding of the culture of each country,

Hendin interviewed attempted suicides, nonsuicidal patients and nurses. The interviews were supplemented with studies of the folklore, literature, drama and cartoons of each country. Based on the information he gathered, Hendin developed a brief description of the motivation for suicide in each of these three Scandinavian countries.

Hendin noted that, in Denmark, mothers often tried to discipline their sons and control their aggression by making them feel guilty. As a result, many Danish men are very dependent on their mothers. Supposedly, this dependency was the root of depression and suicidality after adult experiences of loss or separation, and fantasies of reunion with loved ones were common in suicides.

In Sweden, because parents emphasized performance and success in their children, Swedish children were largely ambitious and work was central to their lives. When men failed in performance, it damaged their self-esteem so significantly that some actually committed suicide. In Norway where the suicide rate was much lower than in Denmark and Sweden, Hendin found the same strong dependency of sons on their mothers, but the Norwegian children appeared more aggressive than Danish children. Alcohol abuse was more common in Norway and the men were more open about their feelings; for example, they were able to laugh at themselves and cry openly. Hendin concluded that the suicide rate was lower in Sweden because the boys stayed out of trouble to please their mothers and because they didn't overly concern themselves with personal failure. In fact they often blame others for their own mistakes and retreat into alcohol abuse rather than suicidal behavior.

Other researchers (Block and Christiansen, 1966) have tried to test Hendin's hypotheses about maternal attitudes by studying the beliefs of students in Denmark, Sweden and Norway. Their study supported Hendin's ideas best for Norway and Denmark and least for Sweden. Evidence was found to support Hendin's suggestions of the importance of competition, maternal authority, physical freedom and autonomy and the use of teasing in child rearing, but not to support the ideas of dependency, toleration for aggressiveness and tolerance for affect.

Farber (1968) also attempted to explain the difference between the Danish and Norwegian suicide rates. Looking at both sociological and psychological variables, he came to these conclusions: (1) Danes view life less hopefully than do Norwegians; (2) Danes have a weaker sense of self-competence than Norwegians; (3) Danes express aggression less easily than Norwegians; (4) Danish neighbors are seen as less succoring than Norwegians; and (5) Danes are more tolerant of suicide than Norwegians. It makes sense that these five conditions could lead to a suicide rate that is higher for Danes than for Norwegians.

SUMMARY

As far as it is possible to tell, genetic factors are not responsible for suicide. Constitutional factors, such as poor health, may predispose a person to suicide. I have also noted that environmental influences, especially those due to cultural factors in child-rearing practices, seem to produce considerable differences in suicidal behavior. When specific cultural practices were examined, logical explanations for those differences were seen. However, we still cannot fully determine whether a culture causes a particular personality pattern in some individuals that leads to suicide, or whether the culture could push a person with any type of personality toward suicide under the right conditions.

REFERENCES

Barraclough, B.M. and Hughes, J. *Suicide*. Beckenham, UK: Croom Helm, 1987.

Block, J. and Christiansen, B. A test of Hendin's hypothesis relating suicide in Scandinavia to child-rearing orientations. *Scandinavian Journal of Psychology* 7:267-268, 1966.

Dorpat, T.L., Anderson, W.F. and Ripley, H.S. The relationship of physical illness to suicide. In H.L.P. Resnik (ed.), *Suicidal Behaviors*, Boston: Little, Brown, 1968.

Farber, M.L. Suicide and the welfare state. *Mental Hygiene* 49:371-373, 1965.

Hendin, H. *Suicide and Scandinavia*. New York: Doubleday, 1965.

Hjortsjo, T. Suicide in relation to somatic illness and complications. *Crisis* 8:125-137, 1987.

Iga, M. *The Thorn in the Chrysanthemum*. Berkeley: University of California Press, 1986.

Kalish, R.A. Suicide. *Bulletin of Suicidology* December 1968, pp. 37-43.

Kallman, F.J. *Heredity in Health and Mental Disease*. New York: W.W. Norton, 1953.

Lester, D. Genetics, twin studies, and suicide. *Suicide and Life-Threatening Behavior* 16:274-295, 1986.

Lester, D. *Suicide as a Learned Behavior*. Springfield, IL: Charles C Thomas, 1987.

Lester, D. *The Biochemical Basis of Suicide*. Springfield, IL: Charles C Thomas, 1988.

Lester, D. *Why People Kill Themselves*. Springfield, IL: Charles C Thomas, 1992.

Lester, D. The concentration of neurotransmitter metabolites in the cerebrospinal fluid of suicidal individuals: a meta-analysis. *Pharmacopsychiatry* 28:45-50, 1995.

Lester, D. and Tallmer, M. *Now I Lay Me Down: Suicide in the Elderly.* Philadelphia: The Charles Press, 1994.

McCandless, F.D. Suicide and the communication of rage. *American Journal of Psychiatry* 125:197-205, 1968.

Naroll, R. *Data Quality Control.* Glencoe, IL: The Free Press, 1962.

Sheldon, W.H. *The Varieties of Temperament.* New York: Harper & Row, 1942.

Thomas, C. and Greenstreet, R. Psychobiological characteristics in youth as predictors of five disease states. *Johns Hopkins Medical Journal* 132:16-43, 1973.

Trautman, E.C. Suicide attempts of Puerto Rican immigrants. *Psychiatric Quarterly* 35:544-554, 1961.

5

Childhood Experiences and Suicide Later in Life

There is no question that unhappy and disorganized childhoods can lead to unhappy and disorganized future lives. This brings us to the question, do particular kinds of unhappy childhoods lead to particular kinds of later unhappy lives? A child's life may be disturbed in many different ways, such as through his parents' marital disharmony, the loss of a parent or by being physically or emotionally abused. This chapter will examine the relationship between particular kinds of childhood disturbances and the tendency of the adult to be suicidal.

FAMILY DISORGANIZATION

One way to tell whether a family is having trouble is to find out whether its members are using community services such as health and welfare agencies or have been involved in court cases. The more difficulty a family is having, the more likely its members will end up in court (whether for crimes or for divorce proceedings), and use public welfare agencies rather than managing their own lives. Some research indicates that suicidal people (especially attempted suicides) more often come from families who used community resources to deal with their problems. Most suicide researchers agree that the suicidal adult probably had a childhood marked by an unusual amount of economic deprivation, neglect and disharmony between his parents. For example, recent research has documented that many suicidal adults grew up in families in which partners had psychiatric problems and were suicidal (Orbach, Gross and Glaubman, 1981), there was conflict among members (Wright, 1985) and parental rejection (Hussain and Vandiver, 1984). In addition, Jacobs (1971) documented that family trauma and disruptions were more extensive for suicidal adolescents than for nonsuicidal adolescents. For example, the mothers of the suicidal adolescents had more often moved and divorced, not just once, but many times.

PUNISHMENT EXPERIENCES

Elsewhere in this book I discuss the concept of inward and outward direction of aggression — the idea that resentment and rage may be expressed by individuals in a characteristic way either by attacks on themselves or on others. This idea was used in the comparative study of suicide and homicide by the sociologists Henry and Short (1954). They suggested that the tendency to turn aggression inward or outward is mostly learned through the experience of punishment during childhood. They concluded that children who are given love-oriented or psychological punishment ("Mommy won't love you if you do that") learn to inhibit their aggression. Because children learn that aggressiveness toward this kind of parent means withdrawal of love, they turn their aggression inward. By contrast, children who are punished physically are not threatened with loss of love so they are not afraid of expressing their aggression outwardly.

Various researchers have tried to test Henry and Short's ideas about aggression with empirical evidence. Gold (1958) suggested that certain groups are more likely than others to have experienced physical punishment as children — males more than females, enlisted men more than officers, rural dwellers more than urban dwellers, and blacks more than whites. If Henry and Short's theory is correct, the first member of each of these groups should show a lower suicide rate than a homicide rate. Gold's findings agreed with this prediction. However, there is always the chance that Gold's broad categories concealed some factor that was actually responsible for the difference in behavior, such as status or educational level.

Two studies (Lester, 1967, 1968) did not support Henry and Short's prediction. First, when examining primitive and nonliterate societies, there seemed to be no correlation between the way children were disciplined and whether they committed suicide or homicide later in life. In the second study, undergraduate students' memories of childhood discipline and their later suicidal tendencies (if any) were investigated, and there seemed to be no association.

Perhaps someday a clear relationship will be shown between suicidal behavior and childhood punishment experiences, but even if this should occur, there would still be questions about a cause-and-effect relationship. The conclusion that punishment experiences cause suicidal behavior would not be proved. Instead, as Bell (1968) has pointed out, children with particular behavioral tendencies may elicit from their parents certain kinds of punishment. A child who responds well to verbal scolding may never be spanked, while another child in the same family may be harder to control and may make the parents feel they have no alternative but to resort to physical punishment. Just as parental behavior can affect the child, the child's behavior can affect the parent.

In recent years, a number of studies have shown that the experience of physical and sexual abuse in childhood and adolescent years is associated with later suicidality (Lester, 1992). In one study, Hibbard, Brack, Rauch and Orr (1988) compared junior high school students who had been abused with students who had not been abused and reported that the abused children had made more suicide attempts and also abused alcohol and ran away from home more often. There are now more than a dozen such reports, but so far the research has not shown whether physical and sexual abuse lead specifically to later suicidal behavior, rather than increasing the incidence of all manner of psychiatric symptoms.

LEONARD'S DEVELOPMENTAL THEORY

C.V. Leonard (1967) has proposed an interesting developmental theory of suicide that has not been empirically tested. She suggested that the second and third years of life were crucial for the development of suicidal tendencies. During those years, children begin their struggle for independence and autonomy from the mother. Their own identities begin to develop. These are difficult tasks and they are made even harder by the fact that the children are still dependent on the mother. Thus the second and third years involve tremendous conflict between the growing desire for autonomy and the fear of alienating the mother while she is still needed.

Leonard believed that the conflict between dependence and independence can be resolved in three ways, each of which is associated with a type of suicidal tendency.

1. People can fail to develop a sense of a separate identity. Their identity may be fused with that of their parents. When intending or wishing to attack the parents, they may turn the violence onto themselves. If their parent dies, they may try to rejoin the loved one by means of suicide.

2. People's development may be blocked so that they do not learn to control their own behavior, but instead rely on external controls to keep them from getting into trouble. Thus, when an

impulse toward suicide is present, these individuals have no techniques for controlling it (such as by reminding themselves that they are afraid to die, or by concentrating on possible future pleasures). If no one else is present to help them, they may yield to the impulse.

3. People may develop only one rigid method of dealing with problems and may lack normal flexibility in handling new situations. When a crisis develops, they are often unable to find a solution, and, in addition, are unwilling to accept compromises.

According to Leonard's theory, the only developmental period in which there is danger of producing a potential suicide is the second and third years of life. Once the child passes safely through this period, he supposedly would be "immunized" against suicide. I suspect that the development of suicidal tendencies may not be this simple, and the remainder of this chapter investigates other ways in which childhood experiences can lead to suicidal behavior.

THE EFFECTS OF PARENTAL DEPRIVATION

An important event to consider when looking at childhood experiences is the loss of a parent through death, divorce or abandonment. Many research studies have attempted to determine the relationship between the loss of a parent and later suicidal behavior. A review of these studies (Lester, 1992) shows that most researchers found an increase in the experience of childhood loss among suicidal individuals. However, the studies differ in two respects: whether loss from the death or from the divorce of parents is the more critical and whether loss of a mother, a father or both parents is more common among suicidal people.

Freud's psychoanalytic theory proposed that loss experienced during the first six years of life would be more traumatic for children than loss experienced when they are older. Lester (1989a) examined the detailed biographies of 30 famous suicides and found loss of a parent or significant other in 15 of the cases. Most of them had lost a father through death when they were between the ages of 6 and 14. It seems, therefore, that loss during any of the childhood and teenage years may increase the risk of later suicidal behavior.

We should remember that losing a parent is a devastating event and we cannot expect a simple cause-and-effect relationship here. The effects of the loss may differ depending on factors such as the nature of the child's previous relationship with his lost parent, as well as his relationship with the remaining parent, the size of the remaining family and the family's economic situation.

One factor that seems to encourage suicide in persons who lost a parent in childhood is the subsequent loss of another important relationship when they became adults. One theory states that early loss may sensitize people to later losses, causing their reaction to be unusually dramatic (Lester and Beck, 1976). Other suicidologists prefer the idea that early loss prevents people from learning how to establish and maintain healthy relationships. They may later become involved in unhealthy relationships that are likelier than others to lead to loss.

THE PARENTAL FAMILIES OF SUICIDAL INDIVIDUALS

What sorts of families do suicides (both attempters and completers) come from? This question covers many issues that are potentially important in the development of suicidal behavior, such as the nature of the relationship between the child's parents and whether the child was wanted. Because there are so many topics to investigate, not much of the research that has yet been done has yielded substantive results. I will discuss only a few of the studies that have been made.

In their investigation, Margolin and Teicher (1968) looked at adolescent boys who had attempted suicide and they noted some general features of the cases. The boys' mothers had often been angry, depressed or withdrawn, both before and after their pregnancy, and they often did not want to become pregnant in the first place. The children frequently experienced some degree of maternal deprivation during their first year of life and the father was often gone by the child's fourth or fifth year of life, leaving the son with no strong male relationships. (This period is considered by psychoanalysts to be a crucial time when the Oedipal conflict is worked out, resulting in the boy's abandonment of fixation on his mother and his identification with his father's social role.) In many of the cases, there was a reversal of traditional roles between mother and son, with the child acting as the "man of the family" and as its head. The sons functioned socially and emotionally as their mothers' "husbands." Many of the boys felt that their mothers did not love them. The child's suicide attempt often came at a time when the mother was depressed and withdrawn and when the son felt rejected or threatened by the loss of his the mother.

Goldney (1981, 1985) found that young women who had attempted suicide were more likely to report that their parents were controlling and less interested and less proud of them. Their homes had more friction and quarrels both between the parents and between the children and the parents. The suicidal women also reported that both of their parents were less caring and more over-protective than the parents of nonsuicidal women.

SIBLING STATUS

The nature of a child's experience within his family may be greatly influenced by whether he is first-born, last-born or a middle child. Often the first-born child gets extra attention from his parents, but because they have never done it before, the parents may be lacking in child-rearing skills. For children born after the first, parents are more experienced in child care, but they may be less interested or too occupied with other children to give much attention. The last-born child, the "baby of the family," may be dependent on his parents much longer than his older siblings were. These differences in childhood experience might lead to differences in suicidal behavior.

Although there is some inconsistency in the many research studies that have been conducted on this topic, a recent review of this research (Lester, 1987) suggested that completed suicide was more common in first-born and middle-born children and that attempted suicide was more common in middle-borns and last-borns.

There are several possible explanations for the preponderance of first-borns among completed suicides. Some researchers (such as Schachter, 1959) have stated that first-born children are unusually dependent on their parents and, when they are under stress, they have a strong need to be with other people. Suicidal behavior can be seen as a "cry for help," a way of moving toward or communicating with others. If this concept is correct (it is still debated), we would expect first-borns to be more frequently involved in suicidal behavior. In addition, if first-borns have learned inappropriate ways of communicating, they might also be very isolated and desperately crave companionship. Their special need for the company of others might interact with their inability to reach other people, causing frustration that could end in suicide.

First-borns differ from later-borns in many ways that could be responsible for their suicidal behavior. For example, because later-borns seem to be physically more vigorous and less hampered by social restraint, they can more easily direct their feelings of aggression outward, compared to first-borns who tend to turn their aggression inward onto themselves.

Middle-born children often feel unloved by parents. The older children get attention because their age enables them to be more successful in most tasks, while younger children, the babies of the family, are often spoiled. As a result, the middle-borns sometimes feel ignored by their parents. (See Lester [1989b] for a case study of a completed suicide in a teenager who was a middle-born child.)

SUICIDES IN THE FAMILY

Do suicides ever come from nonsuicidal families? Do some families seem to have far more than their share of suicidal members? Recent research indicates a tendency for both completed and attempted suicides to have had more suicidal incidents in their families than have nonsuicidal people (Lester, 1992).

Clearly, having a history of suicides in a family could be an experience with a profound effect on a child. They could learn suicidal ways of coping and they could feel that as members of a "suicidal family," they had a special susceptibility to suicide. Also, because suicidal parents are likely to be psychiatrically disturbed, they are equally likely to create an unhealthy environment for raising a child. On the other hand, a high rate of suicide in a family could suggest that the children have genetically inherited a psychiatric disorder that makes suicidal behavior more likely to occur.

Also, the suicide of a particular family member may be especially significant to some other family member; for example, an eldest son might be more affected by the suicide of his father than by that of a younger sister. Both Ernest Hemingway and John Berryman, noted American writers and suicides, had fathers who committed suicide.

SUMMARY

Research has yielded some answers to questions about the contribution of childhood experiences to suicide later in life. It appears that family difficulties during childhood make suicide more likely, especially poor parenting and the experience of physical and sexual abuse. Particular experiences of punishment and problems in a child's development of autonomy from his parent have been singled out as important causal factors, as has the experience of losing a parent. Being the first-born child and coming from a family where suicide has occurred also seem to predispose a person toward suicidal behavior.

REFERENCES

Bell, R.Q. A reinterpretation of the direction of effects in studies of socialization. *Psychological Review* 75:81-95, 1968.

Gold, M. Suicide, homicide, and the socialization of aggression. *American Journal Sociology* 63:651-661, 1958.

Goldney, R.D. Parental loss and reported childhood stress in young women who attempted suicide. *Acta Psychiatrica Scandinavica* 64:34-49, 1981.

Goldney, R.D. Parental representation in young women who attempted suicide. *Acta Psychiatrica Scandinavica* 72:230-232, 1985.

Henry, A.F. and Short, J.F. *Suicide and Homicide.* Glencoe, IL: The Free Press, 1954.

Hibbard, R.A., Brack, C.J., Rauch, S. and Orr, D.P. Abuse, feelings and health behavior in a student population. *American Journal of Diseases in Children* 142:326-330, 1988.

Hussain, S.A., and Vandiver, T. *Suicide in Children and Adolescents.* New York: Spectrum, 1984.

Jacobs, J. *Adolescent Suicide.* New York: Wiley, 1971.

Leonard, C.V. *Understanding and Preventing Suicide.* Springfield, IL: Charles C Thomas, 1967.

Lester, D. Suicide, homicide, and the effects of socialization. *Journal of Personality and Social Psychology* 5:466-468, 1967.

Lester, D. Punishment experiences and suicidal preoccupation. *Journal of Genetic Psychology* 113:89-94, 1968.

Lester, D. Suicide and sibling position. *Individual Psychology* 43:390-395, 1987.

Lester, D. Experience of parental loss and later suicide. *Acta Psychiatrica Scandinavica* 79:450-452, 1989a.

Lester, D. Suicide in a middle-born child. *Adolescence* 245:909-914, 1989b.

Lester, D. *Why People Kill Themselves.* Springfield, IL: Charles C Thomas, 1992.

Lester, D. and Beck, A.T. Early loss as a possible sensitizer to later loss in attempted suicides. *Psychological Reports* 39:121-122, 1976.

Margolin, N.L. and Teicher, J.D. Thirteen adolescent male suicide attempters. *Journal of the American Academy of Child Psychiatry* 7:296-315, 1968.

Orbach, I., Gross, Y. and Glaubman, H. Some common characteristics of latency-age suicidal children. *Suicide and Life-Threatening Behavior* 11:180-190, 1981.

Schachter, S. *The Psychology of Affiliation.* Stanford, CA: Stanford University Press, 1959.

Wright, L. Suicidal thoughts and their relationship to family stress and personal problems among high school seniors and college undergraduates. *Adolescence* 20:575-580, 1985.

6

Personality and Suicide

The term "personality" describes the complex behavioral and emotional characteristics that distinguish an individual from all other people. Thus, not all behaviors are considered to be a part of a person's personality. For example, eating food is a trait that all people have in common with other humans, so it is not a personality factor. Personality does come into play when we look at how much a person eats, what he eats and when he eats, because these are all factors on which people may differ.

Having noted the distinctions above, readers should not expect this chapter to concentrate on psychoanalytic personality components or the results of psychological testing. Instead, I will examine a number of areas of behavior whose relation to suicide has been tested. These will range from intelligence level to sleeping habits.

SUICIDAL TYPES

I will begin by considering general attempts to classify types of suicidal people in terms of their needs or motivations. Suicide is a very complex behavior and every suicidal person is different. In keeping with the generally agreed-upon premise that suicide does not occur at random, suicidologists have defined general categories into which suicidal people can be placed.

Karl Menninger (1938) formulated one of the earliest and best known of these classifications. He felt that there were three basic motivations for suicide: the wish to die, the wish to kill and the wish to be killed. People who wish to die essentially want to escape from something unpleasant in their lives; they may be in a state of chronic physiological or psychological suffering. People who wish to kill may see suicide as an act of revenge and as a way of inflicting guilt and suffering on other people. Finally, suicidal people who wish to be killed may be seeking punishment for an act or for thoughts that they consider wrong.

Menninger believed that all three motives played some part in every suicide, although it is possible to identify suicides that seem to show one primary motive. The following suicide notes are written by people who seem to have one primary motive: the wish to die, the wish to kill or the wish to be killed.

Dear Mary — You have been the best wife a man could want and I still love you after fifteen years. Don't think too badly of me for taking this way out but I can't take much more pain and sickness. Also I may get too much pain or so weak that I can't go this easy way. With all my love forever — Bill (Shneidman and Farberow, 1956, p. 203).

Bill: I do hope you'll suffer more than I have done. I wish you'll die in a beer joint (Wagner, 1960, p. 63).

Mary Darling, It's all my fault. I've thought this over a million times and this seems to be the only way I can settle all the trouble I have caused you and others. This is only a sample of how sorry I am. This should cancel all (Shneidman and Farberow, 1956, p. 206).

Shneidman (1968) has suggested a very different classification system, based on the source of the suicidal person's problems. He described the following three kinds of suicide. *Egotic* suicides are those in which the primary problem comes from conflicts within the person. People with an egotic suicide pattern may have a strong need for some sort of satisfaction, but an equally strong inhibition against seeking it. *Dyadic* suicides are those that stem from conflicts with other people. *Ageneratic* suicides are those that result from a sense of alienation, when a person loses his sense of continuity and participation in the succession of human generations.

Another approach to the classification of suicides involves the description of syndromes rather than single motives toward suicide. A few of the suicidal syndromes that have been described follow:

1. *The Discarded Woman* (Peck, 1968). The individual feels abandoned, rejected and finally suicidal after the loss of a loved one.

2. *The Adolescent Crisis* (Peck, 1968). A young person becomes suicidal in response to family issues, such as those centered around his own dependency needs or attempts to establish a sense of identity.

3. *The Malignant Masochist* (Pretzel, 1968). The suicidal person has a history of suicide attempts and dedicates much of her life to self-punishment.

4. *The Harlequin* (Pretzel, 1968). This syndrome is named after the character in medieval drama who is both Death and a seducer. (The concept can be traced back to the story of Pluto's abduction of Persephone.) The harlequin is much like the malignant masochist, but in addition he personifies and gives an erotic component to the idea of death.

IMPULSIVENESS

In a discussion of personality correlates of suicidal behavior, the consideration of impulsiveness is important. The inability to resist sudden whims could lead to suicidal behavior, just as it could lead to many other rash acts. Students who have attempted or threatened suicide seem to be more irritable and more impulsive than nonsuicidal students (Lester, 1967). In a study of people who poisoned themselves but did not die from their act, Kessel (1966) judged about two-thirds of the acts to be impulsive; although these people had most likely thought about suicide at some time in the past, they had not been focusing on it before they poisoned themselves. The impulse "just came over them," and they yielded to it at once. Williams' group (1980) found that 40 percent of a sample of attempted suicides had premeditated the act for less than five minutes! Impulsive suicide attempts such as these are less likely to be fatal than carefully planned ones and this may be due in part to the fact that the impulsive attempter does not really want to die. The impulsive attempters in Williams' study frequently informed someone of their impending suicidal act and orchestrated the situation so that others could observe them in the act, thereby facilitating intervention.

ATTITUDES TOWARD DEATH

The many different metaphors that people use to describe death suggest that there are many different attitudes about death. For example, death may be seen as a horrific event that should be put out of one's mind as long as possible. It may also be seen as a means of escape from an unpleasant existence, a way to avoid "the slings and arrows of outrageous fortune." It may be considered as a quiet and dignified exit for those who have lived good lives, but a fearful punishment for the profligate and the wicked. Clearly these attitudes and the plethora of other ways of seeing death will be affected by an individual's beliefs in the existence and nature of an afterlife.

One might expect that people's attitudes about death would influence their readiness to kill themselves. Considerable research has been done on the effect of this personality variable on suicidal behavior. Some of the research methods that have been used include asking subjects to classify the concepts of life and death as positive or negative, asking subjects in a questionnaire to agree or disagree with statements about death and testing subjects' physiological responses to words relating to death or suicide.

Orbach and associates (1984) have found that suicidal children have more of an aversion to life and less of an aversion to death than nonsuicidal children, and Pfeffer (1989-90) has found that suicidal children are more preoccupied with death than nonsuicidal children. Although some real relationships may exist between views of death and suicide, correlations may be different for men and women, for people of different ages and for attempted and completed suicides. As long as studies do not carefully handle these groups separately, it will be difficult to find a consistent relationship between suicide and attitudes toward death.

HOPE

A factor that may be more important than a person's attitude toward death in influencing his tendency toward suicide is his attitude toward life; in other words, the degree of hope he has about his own life situation. One suicide researcher has suggested that people who commit suicide are more negative about life than they are positive about death. Ganzler (1967, p. 95) says that suicidal people feel as if they are

> ...being driven from life, into a state of non-being, which they
> designate as not being alive. At least on a semantic level, it is
> not so much that the suicidal person is pulled toward death as
> a positive, desired state so much as he feels the need to remove
> himself from a painful and meaningless life.

Farber (1968) has tried to analyze the degree of hope about life in terms of the "sense of competence" postulated by Robert White (1959). White believes that a sense of competence is the basis of all human motivation. Simply put, it is the feeling of being able to make some change in the environment, of being able to control the world, and, by implication, of being sure that the world will satisfy one's needs. According to Farber's theory, some personalities may increase their risk of suicide because of a chronically reduced sense of self-competence. Others will become suicidal when some change in the social environment causes their feeling of competence to diminish. When the latter event occurs, there is the threat that the individual will not be able to sustain a minimally acceptable existence. Possible changes that could bring this about include abandonment by a loved one, the loss of a job or one's fortune, or a life-threatening disease.

People's sense of their competence and the threats to an acceptable life condition determine their level of hope, and the greater it is, the less the likelihood that they will commit suicide. A person's level of hope is increased when his feeling of competence increases, but it is decreased when acceptable life conditions are increasingly threatened. If people have a strong sense of self-competence, a serious threat to their life conditions will be needed before the probability of suicide increases. If they start out with a minimal sense of competence, however, a trivial threat to life conditions might be enough to make suicide a serious possibility.

Empirical research has supported Farber's ideas. In recent years, hopelessness has become one of the strongest correlates of suicidal preoccupation and behavior. For example, Lester's group (1975) found that the more serious the suicidal intent of attempted suicides (as measured by their self-report or by the objective circumstances of their suicidal act), the higher they score on a psychological measure of hopelessness. In addition, in a follow-up study (Lester et al., 1979), those who went on to kill themselves in the next five years were among the most hopeless in the initial study.

SELF-CONCEPT

An important variable in determining the likelihood that people will commit suicide may be the way in which they think of themselves — their self-concept. If they consider themselves worthless and guilty, there may be an increase in what Menninger called the wish to be killed. There are a number of ways to determine people's self-concept. A tester can give subjects a list of adjectives and ask them to choose the words that most relate to them; they can simply be asked to describe themselves; or they can be asked to choose adjectives that describe how they would like to be, and then compare them to the way they think they really are. These methods have yielded some information about the self-concept of the suicidal person.

In general, suicidal people have lower self-esteem than nonsuicidal people (Lester, 1992). For example, Kaplan (1978) found that the level of self-concept predicted which seventh-grade children in a school system would attempt suicide in the following year.

Miller (1968) explored a number of aspects of self-concept that seem relevant to suicidal behavior. She postulated that seriously suicidal people are overcommitted to some hero-image that even though they are unable to emulate, they can never abandon. Potentially, suicidal people are also unable to communicate well with their loved ones, so the latter cannot help them to deal with their problems. Such people are isolated by their inability to communicate and spend their time castigating themselves for failing to achieve the status they want. A minor event can then trigger a crisis if it seems relevant to the conflict the individuals are feeling about their ideal self. They may see themselves as failures, as worthless, and as better off dead. Miller's empirical studies supported these ideas. The suicidal people she studied seemed to be more negative about themselves than nonsuicidal people. They were also more rigid and authoritarian, more prone to have crises and more inclined to have problems communicating with others.

THE PRE-SUICIDAL MOOD

Most theories of suicide assume that depression immediately precedes a suicidal act. Indeed suicidal individuals are frequently found to have a depressive disorder (as a primary or secondary diagnosis), and such individuals typically obtain high scores on psychological measures of depression (Lester, 1992).

However, there seems to be a tendency for the depression (as well as any confusion and anxiety) to clear up shortly before the suicidal act, so that during the preceding day or so the suicidal individual may appear calm and even optimistic (Clements et al., 1985). This may be due to an improvement of mood once the decision to commit suicide has been made. On the other hand, as Spiegel and Neuringer (1963) have pointed out, it may be that suicidal people must repress their awareness of their suicidal desires in order to be able to kill themselves. If they were aware of their suicidal intent, the fear of death attendant upon considering suicide would make it more difficult for them to carry out the act. This process may be responsible for the euphoric mood that often immediately precedes a suicidal act.

REASONS FOR LIVING

In an interesting departure from most research on suicide, Linehan and co-workers (1983) focused on personal attitudes that might *prevent* people from committing suicide, rather than concentrating on those characteristics that might increase suicidal risk. They devised a "Reasons for Living" questionnaire and, from the responses they got, identified six major reasons why people decide *not* to commit suicide: (1) survival and coping beliefs, in other words, confidence in their ability to handle and survive the crisis; (2) responsibility to their families, both material and psychological (e.g., sparing family members grief); (3) child-related concerns, especially the psychological effect that their suicide might have on their children; (4) fear of suicide, including the pain involved and the consequences of life after death; (5) fear of social disapproval; and (6) moral objections based on their religion and their personal philosophy of life. Linehan's research showed that responses to the "Reasons for Living" questionnaire could predict suicidal behavior in that respondents who were more strongly committed to these reasons for living were less likely to engage in suicidal behavior.

PSYCHOLOGICAL TESTS

The frequency with which psychological tests are used as diagnostic instruments reflects a somewhat misplaced faith in their usefulness. Newspaper write-ups about the arrest of a disturbed person often end with the statement that the individual "was sent to the state hospital for psychological testing." The implication is that the tests will reveal exactly where the individual's problems lie and, therefore, how he can be restored to health. To argue with this general belief in psychological testing is far beyond the scope of this book, but I can say that research indicates very little usefulness for standard psychological evaluations, such as intelligence tests and inkblot tests, in the prediction of suicidal behavior (Lester, 1970, 1992).

SUMMARY

Suicidologists have described a number of general suicidal patterns or types. They have also looked at the relation between specific personality characteristics (such as hope and self-concept) and suicidal behavior. To sum these up, we can characterize suicidal people as unusually rigid and inflexible, usually depressed, with a negative view of themselves and a positive view of death, lacking in hope and with few acknowledged reasons for staying alive.

REFERENCES

Clements, C., Bonacci, D., Yerevanian, B., Privitera, M. and Kiehne, L. Assessment of suicide risk in patients with personality disorder and major affective disorder. *Quality Review Bulletin* 11(5):150-154, 1985.

Farber, M.L. *Theory of Suicide.* New York: Funk & Wagnalls, 1968.

Ganzler, S. Some interpersonal and social dimensions of suicidal behavior. *Dissertation Abstracts* 28B:1192-1193, 1967.

Kaplan, H.B. Self-attitudes and multiple modes of deviance. In D. Lettieri (ed.) *Drugs and Suicide.* Beverly Hills, CA: Sage, 1978.

Kessel, N. The respectability of self-poisoning and the fashion of survival. *Journal of Psychosomatic Research* 10:29-36, 1966.

Lester, D. Resentment and dependency in the suicidal individual. *Journal of General Psychology* 81:137-145, 1967.

Lester, D. Attempts to predict suicidal risk using psychological tests. *Psychological Bulletin* 74:1-17, 1970.

Lester, D. *Why People Kill Themselves.* Springfield, IL: Charles C Thomas, 1992.

Lester, D., Beck, A.T. and Mitchell, B. Extrapolation from attempted suicide to completed suicide. *Journal of Abnormal Psychology* 88:78-80, 1979.

Lester, D., Beck, A.T. and Trexler, L. Extrapolation from attempted suicides to completed suicides. *Journal of Abnormal Psychology* 84:563-566, 1975.

Linehan, M.M., Goodstein, J.L., Nielsen, S.L. and Chiles, J.A. Reasons for staying alive when you're thinking of killing yourself. *Journal of Consulting and Clinical Psychology* 51:276-286, 1983.

Menninger, K. *Man Against Himself.* New York: Harcourt, Brace & World, 1938.

Miller, D.H. Suicidal careers. *Dissertation Abstracts* 28A:4720, 1968.

Orbach, I., Feshbach, S., Carlson, G. and Ellenberg, L. Attitudes toward life and death in suicidal, normal and chronically ill children. *Journal of Consulting and Clinical Psychology* 52:1020-1027, 1984.

Peck, M.L. Two suicide syndromes. Paper presented at the American Psychological Association meeting, San Francisco, 1968.

Pfeffer, C. Preoccupations with death in "normal" children. *Omega* 20:205-212, 1989-90.

Pretzel, P.W. Two suicide syndromes. Paper presented at the American Psychological Association meeting, San Francisco, 1968.

Shneidman, E.S. Classification of suicidal phenomena. *Bulletin of Suicidology,* July 1968, pp. 1-9.

Shneidman, E.S. and Farberow, N.L. *Clues to Suicide.* New York: McGraw-Hill, 1957.

Spiegel, D.E. and Neuringer, C. Role of dread in suicidal behavior. *Journal of Abnormal and Social Psychology* 66:507-511, 1963.

Wagner, F.F. Suicide notes. *Danish Medical Bulletin* 7:62-64, 1960.

White, R.W. Motivation reconsidered. *Psychological Review* 16:297-333, 1959.

Williams, C., Davidson, J. and Montgomery, I. Impulsive suicidal behavior. *Journal of Clinical Psychology* 36:90-94, 1980.

7

Aggression and Suicide

Many research workers believe that suicide is a form of aggression. If killing or hurting another person is an example of an act of aggression, it follows that killing or hurting oneself is also an act of aggression. Some researchers believe that it is necessary to go beyond this simple analogy; they feel that even though most people have approximately the same amount of aggression, most everyone differs in the way they direct this tendency. Whether a person behaves suicidally or not is partly determined by the way he directs his aggressive energies at a particular time.

Freud was the first person to apply this approach to the problem of suicide. He never actually considered the psychodynamics of suicide in detail, but he did refer to it occasionally in his writings. Freud's comments were based on his considerable experience with suicidal patients and also possibly on his personal interest in suicide. (Many people feel that Freud was preoccupied with his own death. He once threatened to kill himself if he were to lose his fiancée and he frequently made predictions, all of which were incorrect, about the date of his own death. He also refused to stop smoking cigars long after being diagnosed with cancer.) Litman (1967), who compiled Freud's written comments about suicide, noted that Freud outlined two stages that he believed led to suicidal behavior. First of all, some loved object is lost. The emotional investment that had previously been directed to the object of love is withdrawn and reinvested within the self. Along with this reinvestment of feeling, the loved one is recreated as a permanent part of the self, becoming a kind of ideal self. This is called identification of the ego with the lost object. Litman called this process ego-splitting, because the self is divided into an ideal and a nonideal self. Secondly, the individual redirects toward himself the aggression that he feels about the outside world. He feels resentment and anger toward the lost object of his love, but there is no way to express these strong feelings to the

55

love object because it is no longer present. Aggression is therefore turned toward the only remaining representation of the love object — the ideal self. In killing or destroying the ideal self, however, the suicidal person also kills his physical self.

Many psychologists and sociologists have used this idea of suicide as aggression turned inward and onto the self, in contrast to the act of homicide, for example, which is an act of outward-directed aggression. Henry and Short (1954) suggested that people become inwardly or outwardly aggressive depending on the way they were punished as children. Menninger (1938) suggested that feelings of anger at other people were one of three major motivations for suicide (along with the desire to punish oneself and the desire to escape from pain).

Henry and Short believe that children whose parents use love-oriented punishment techniques (e.g., threatening to withdraw their love or companionship) will direct their aggression inward. Most children will feel anger in response to this type of punishment, but because they are afraid that showing this anger might result in the threatened loss of love, they feel they must inhibit their resentment. The child therefore learns not to express aggression outwardly. This does not necessarily mean that the aggression is gone; if we assume it still exists and must be expressed in some way, we have to conclude that the only direction the aggressive feelings can take is inward.

Henry and Short expect children whose parents use physical punishment to demonstrate outwardly directed aggression. When the child responds to his parents with anger, the worst consequence he can expect is a spanking, not the catastrophic withdrawal of the parents' love. These children learn that the outward expression of aggression is not totally unacceptable and they grow up to direct their aggression outward.

These analyses of the sources of inward and outward aggression sound quite logical; however, unfortunately, there is little empirical evidence to support them and the "face" validity of a theory is no substitute for solid evidence. Let us look at some recent "hard" research that may shed light on the idea of suicide as a form of aggression.

SUICIDE AS INWARD-DIRECTED AGGRESSION

Do we have research that shows that suicidal people inhibit their aggression? One study (Lester, 1967) focused on the aggressive behavior of a group of students who had differing histories of suicidal preoccupation (some had threatened or attempted suicide and others had never considered suicide). When frustrated, none of the students differed in the extent to which they showed or inhibited their aggression (attacking others, destroying objects, verbally abusing others). Students with differing degrees of suicidal preoccupation reported similar aggressive habits. From this study, it appears that suicidal people do not inhibit their aggression.

One psychological test that attempts to measure people's aggressive responses to frustration is the Rosenzweig Picture-Frustration Test (Rosenzweig et al., 1947). This test presents a series of cartoons that depict two characters, one of whom is frustrating the other. The test subjects are asked to write a verbal reply for the victim. The responses to the test can be categorized as extrapunitive (aggression is directed toward others), intropunitive (aggression is directed toward themselves) and impunitive (no aggression is directed). Psychologists have given this test to people right after they attempted to kill themselves and in some cases found evidence that these attempters respond differently than nonsuicidal people who, even though not suicidal, are as emotionally disturbed as the suicide attempters. For example, Farmer and Creed (1986) found that attempters were more extrapunitive and intropunitive than the nonattempters and this was especially true of the attempters who were depressed.

There is considerable clinical evidence to support the notion that suicidal people are actually outwardly aggressive. Farberow and his colleagues (1966) looked at the case records of a group of psychiatric patients who killed themselves and found that they had displayed a good deal of violence during times that they were hospitalized. They needed physical restraints more often than the nonsuicidal patients and they also got into more fist fights.

In a study of psychiatric patients (Plutchik, Van Praag and Conte, 1989), researchers found an association between the risk of suicidal behavior and the risk of violent behavior. Both suicide and violent behavior were predicted by similar psychological variables, including depression, hopelessness, impulsivity, a poor social network, and for women, severe menstrual problems.

Tardiff and Sweillam (1980, 1981) found that almost half of a group of psychiatric patients who had attempted suicide in the past three months had also assaulted others. The assaultive suicidal patients more often had symptoms of schizophrenia, disturbed relationships with family members and friends, as well as higher levels of anger and irritation.

SUMMARY

From the available research, it is fairly clear that we cannot make the simple determination that suicidal people tend to turn their aggression inward or that they are not aggressive, as opposed to those who turn their aggression outward. Indeed, those who have attempted and completed suicide often have a history of making attacks on other people and various studies have shown that this group does not inhibit aggression. Despite this fact, many psychotherapists who work with suicidal patients continue to believe that the hypothesis of inward-directed aggression provides them with a good framework. Some researchers believe that the direction in which aggression turns is determined by the way people were punished as children by their parents. While these ideas seem to be very logical, there is little empirical evidence to support them. In fact, some research indicates that suicidal people do not inhibit their aggression and that they are actually outwardly aggressive.

REFERENCES

Farberow, N.L., Shneidman, E.S. and Neuringer, C. Case history and hospitalization factors in suicides of neuropsychiatric hospital patients. *Journal of Nervous and Mental Disease* 142:32-44, 1966.

Farmer, R.D. and Creed, F. Hostility and deliberate self-poisoning. *British Journal of Medical Psychology* 59:311-316, 1986.

Henry, A.F. and Short, J.F. *Suicide and Homicide*. Glencoe, IL: The Free Press, 1954.

Lester, D. Suicide as an aggressive act. *Journal of Psychology* 66:47-50, 1967.

Litman, R.E. Sigmund Freud on suicide. In E.S. Shneidman (ed.), *Essays in Self-Destruction*. New York: Science House, 1967.

Menninger, K. *Man Against Himself*. New York: Harcourt Brace & World, 1938.

Plutchik, R., Van Praag, H.M. and Conte, H.R. Correlates of suicide and violence risk. *Psychiatry Research* 28:215-225, 1989.

Rosenzweig, S., Fleming, E.E. and Clarke, H.J. Revised scoring manual for the Rosenzweig Picture-Frustration Study. *Journal of Psychology* 24:169-205, 1947.

Tardiff, K. The risk of assaultive behavior in suicidal patients. *Acta Psychiatrica Scandinavica* 64:295-300, 1981.

Tardiff, K., and Sweillam, A. Factors related to increased risk of assaultive behavior in suicidal patients. *Acta Psychiatrica Scandinavica* 62:63-68, 1980.

8

Suicide and Homicide

There are various similarities between the motivations for killing oneself and killing another person. Both acts can be effective ways of satisfying certain needs such as revenge, self-punishment and the release of feelings of hostility. A person who wants revenge can get it either by killing someone else or by killing himself and making another person feel guilt about having a possible responsibility for his suicide. An individual who wants to be punished can kill himself or gain the disapproval and punishment of society by killing someone else. Both suicide and homicide may be considered as ways of releasing or draining off hostility.

Because there are similarities in the motives behind suicide and homicide, it would be logical to assume that there would also be a relationship between the occurrences of the two acts. For example, if the two events are alternative and opposing ways of achieving the same end, we would expect them to be negatively correlated; that is, groups of people with a high homicide rate would be expected to have a low incidence of suicide and vice versa. In this chapter, we will investigate the research that has been conducted and the theories that have been formulated about the relationship between suicide and homicide.

CORRELATES OF SUICIDE AND HOMICIDE
ACROSS SOCIETIES

The relationship between the suicide and homicide rate in a society appears to depend entirely on the type of area being studied. For example, in one international study, nations with a high quality of life and a low birth rate had a high suicide rate and a low homicide rate (Lester, 1995). In a study of the United States (excluding Alaska and Hawaii), Lester (1994) found a different set of predictors for the states that had high suicide rates than he did for the states with high homicide rates. For example, he found that when social integration was low (high divorce rates and large percentages of migrants), suicide rates were high, and in the South, homicide rates were high. The same sort of differences by region in the occurrence of these acts have been identified in older research; for example, Halbwachs (1930) found that the Catholic provinces of Germany had a high nonfatal assault rate and a low suicide rate; that Protestant provinces had a high suicide rate and a low assault rate; and that provinces that had no dominant religion had equal rates of both. In France, in contrast, the regions that had a high suicide rate also had a high assault rate.

These very mixed results suggest that the relationship between suicide and homicide is too complex to analyze through crude measures that group together people of all ages, cultural backgrounds and motivations. For some subgroups of the population (such as whites and African Americans), suicide and homicide might be alternative choices, whereas they may not be for other subgroups (such as men and women).

SUICIDAL MURDERERS

In order to determine the nature of the relationship between suicide and homicide, we must try to identify the differences between the kinds of people who commit each act. Generally speaking, people who commit murder are different from people who commit suicide in terms of age, race and gender (Pokorny, 1965). There are, however, some people who commit both acts — sometimes within a time period of only minutes or hours.

In 1966, West discovered that one-third of the murderers he was studying had also gone on to kill themselves soon after killing their victims. He also found that some murderers made unsuccessful attempts to kill themselves, but this is difficult to document. West discovered that some of his subjects had longstanding histories of violent behavior and that they had high levels of aggression. He believed that depending on the circumstances, they either turned this aggression against others or they turned it toward themselves. The following case is typical of those reported by West.

> The offender was an excitable, talkative, boastful man of low intelligence. He was constantly unemployed on account of symptoms of backache, which were considered by hospital doctors to be largely hysterical. He was referred to a psychiatrist and put on a tranquilizer. He was in severe conflict with his wife and various authorities had been approached to inter-

vene on account of his violence toward her and his children. He was described by a family doctor as 'a pale little man, full of resentments against the world and immensely aggressive.' He so resented interference that when his baby had pneumonia he turned out of the house the doctor who called to examine the child. He was reported to have been so irritated by his baby crying during a fatal illness that he picked it up and threw it across the room. His wife had been seen by social workers badly bruised and with a tooth knocked out following arguments with her husband, and on another occasion he had attacked his wife in a very frightening way in the presence of a social worker who had called about the children.

Six weeks before the murder, the offender's wife finally left the home, and two children remained behind. He made numerous threats that unless she returned he would kill the children and himself. Finally, he did so, leaving behind a note blaming his wife (West, 1966, pp. 83-84).

Combined murder-suicide is a relatively common phenomenon in England. It appears that the murderer who also commits suicide is a very different sort of person than the murderer who does not subsequently kill himself. The former is likely to kill a close relative, a spouse or a child. Instead of using brutal methods like stabbing or strangulation, he usually prefers methods that allow him to kill at a distance, like shooting or asphyxiating with gas (West, 1966), perhaps because distance makes the job less personal.

Women are more likely to commit murder/suicide than they are to commit just murder. Of the murderers in West's study, 40 percent of all murder/suicides were committed by women as opposed to 12 percent who only committed murder. In the United States, suicide by women who have just murdered their young children is quite common. Their main motivation is delusional altruism — that the children would suffer if their mother committed suicide and left them alone (Resnick, 1969).

It appears that the suicidal murderers studied by West did not kill themselves to escape punishment for the murder they had just committed and, in many cases, the suicides seemed to have been motivated by despair rather than hostility. Many of the murders involved infanticides, mercy killings and possible death pacts. Other cases appeared to have been accidental killings followed by the suicide of the grief-stricken killer.

In his study of murder-suicides in the United States, Dorpat (1966) found that, in many cases, the two people knew each other and that there was a lot of conflict in their relationship. Many of the murders occurred after a real or a threatened separation. Dorpat suggested that the idea of separation was so frightening to the murderer that his ability to cope regressed to an almost infantile stage in which he had trouble differentiating between himself and the object of his love. Aggression produced by the conflict with the beloved person can be directed either toward the self or toward the other. A suicide following a murder could also represent an acting out of reunion fantasies: after killing a loved one, the murderer may wish that the dead person could be restored to him. The murder occurred in the first place because of a conflict between love and hate, and the feelings of love were not destroyed along with the person's life. The murderer might then wish to rejoin the person he has killed and attempt to do so by means of his own death.

Findings about murder-suicides in the United States have been somewhat different from those in England. Whereas the English murder-suicides studied usually were apparently based on despair rather than hostility or guilt, research on American suicides indicates that they often seemed to kill themselves because of overwhelming guilt. Marvin Wolfgang (1958) compared wives who had killed their husbands and husbands who had killed their wives. He found that 10 of the 53 husbands subsequently killed themselves, while only 1 of 47 wives did so. This difference was attributed to differences in guilt felt after the murder. Wolfgang hypothesized that the murdered husbands were more likely to have prompted their deaths by provoking their wives (e.g., with physical force). As a result, the wives would feel that the murder had been justified to some extent and so they would be less likely to feel guilt and therefore less likely to kill themselves as self-punishment for the murder.

In Wolfgang's (1957) discussion of murder-suicide, he rightly points out that it is difficult to tell whether a person felt excessive guilt before killing himself. However, the murderers in Wolfgang's investigation had fewer previous arrests than the nonsuicidal murderers, and perhaps this indicated that they were more concerned with conformity and obedience to the law. A serious crime like murder might make these people feel such unbearable guilt that only suicide could overcome it.

When considering the role of guilt in the murder-suicide, we should think about two aspects of conscience or superego: the ability to resist temptation and the tendency to feel guilt when a rule has been broken. In *Suicide and Homicide* (1954), Henry and Short suggest that people who complete suicide after committing a murder have strong superegos — that is, they seriously internalize society's prohibitions. By killing themselves, they are carrying out society's rule that a transgressor must be punished. One might ask, however, if the person's belief in obeying the law was not strong enough to prevent the murder in the first place, how could the breaking of the law produce strong enough guilt to cause suicide?

An experiment in training dogs with different punishment techniques may shed some light on how people develop feelings of guilt (Richard Solomon, cited in Mowrer, 1960). In this experiment, dogs were trained to avoid horsemeat (which they like) and, instead, to eat dry dog food. One group of dogs received a smack on the nose whenever they would approach the horsemeat, but before they had a chance to begin eating. These dogs developed such a strong resistance to temptation that they rarely touched the meat even when no one was watching. If they did touch the horsemeat, they showed little emotional reaction or guilt. The other group of dogs were punished just after they began eating the horsemeat. These dogs developed little resistance to temptation, but if they broke the rule and ate the meat, they showed emotional distress or guilt.

This experiment suggests that perhaps the punishment process should be studied with respect to aggression. Perhaps the murderers who do not commit suicide were punished as children for thinking about expressing aggression outwardly rather than after the aggression had begun. As adults, they may attack another person only under extreme provocation, but feel no guilt afterwards. Murderers who do commit suicide, on the other hand, may have been punished only after the act of aggression had begun.

Another type of murder-suicide that has recently been noted is when an elderly person suffering from a chronic or terminal illness is killed by a loving partner who then tries to kill himself. Sometimes the murderer is unsuccessful and is charged with murder. Sometimes both partners form a pact to commit suicide (as in the case of the English-Hungarian writer Arthur Koestler and his wife Cynthia), while in other cases one partner assumes the responsibility for the entire task and the other partner takes a passive or unwitting role.

VICTIM-PRECIPITATED HOMICIDE

In the previous section, it was mentioned that murders sometimes occur because of the deliberately provocative behavior of a person who wants to be killed, in other words, antagonizing another person so seriously that murder results, for example. In his study of homicide in Philadelphia, Wolfgang (1959) estimated that the victim had precipitated his own murder in 26 percent of the cases.

Wolfgang believed that the murder victims who provoked their killers were suicide-prone, but that they differed from other suicides in the extent to which they had internalized the behavioral standards of society; in other words, they had low ethical standards for their own behavior. The guilt they felt when they were not honest, for example, was diffuse and not clearly felt at a conscious level.

Whether a person completes suicide or provokes someone else into killing him may depend on the subculture in which he lives. If his cultural group offers him more exposure to suicide than homicide, he may choose suicide and greater exposure to homicide may cause him to provoke someone else to kill him. In the Philadelphia study, for example, the white/black ratio was 9:1 for completed suicides, 2:1 for victim-precipitated homicides and 3:7 for ordinary homicides, statistics that clearly mirror the behaviors that are characteristic of each subculture.

THE CHOICE BETWEEN SUICIDE AND HOMICIDE

Even though murder and suicide are sometimes committed by one person, most people who commit murder are quite different from people who commit suicide. How do people become murderers or, alternatively, suicides? The sociologists A.F. Henry and J.F. Short (1954) developed a theory that attempts to explain how one or the other of these aggressive orientations evolve. They assumed that the main target of aggression for most people is another person; for others, the target becomes the self. This "decision," they felt, depends on the individual's childhood experiences.

Two sources that may be important in determining how children learn to direct their aggression are the sociological pressures they are subject to and their psychological characteristics. In terms of sociological pressures, a primary factor may be the strength of external restraint that is enforced on the child. If children are forced to conform rigidly to other people's demands, then, in the eyes of the child, these other people are responsible for the consequences of the child's behavior. If, later in life, this person becomes frustrated or annoyed, even with himself, he will strike out against other people because he has learned that others are responsible for his behavior. On the other hand, when a child is subject to very few restraints, when he becomes frustrated as an adult, generally he will not strike out against others.

Henry and Short found that there are two psychological correlates of the tendency to orient aggression toward others: low guilt combined with superego strength (i.e., "conscience" or resistance to temptation), and a particular type of cardiovascular reaction that occurs during stress. Henry and Short's evidence indicates that, for the male child, these two factors are associated with having experienced physical instead of love-oriented punishment by the father rather than by the mother. Presumably, outward-directed aggression, a tendency that is present from birth, continues if punishment is physical. On the other hand, when punishment involves a threatened loss of love the child cannot react with aggression against the frustrator. If he does, he risks further or permanent loss of love from his primary source of nurturance.

As mentioned in Chapter 7, there is no hard research evidence for the common assumption that suicide is an act of inward-directed aggression, although the idea makes good clinical sense. This is a serious problem for Henry and Short's theory. Nevertheless, in spite of this basic objection, a number of researchers have tested some of the predictions of the theory.

One prediction that can be derived from Henry and Short's theory is that suicide should be more common in social groups that have a great deal of freedom of action than in groups in which behavior is seriously constrained by the rest of society. People in the latter groups would be expected to commit more murders, because environmental pressure would have encouraged them to assign responsibility to other people and to express aggression outwardly. In the United States, murders should then be more frequent among the lower classes and racial minorities, whereas suicide should be more frequent among the white upper classes. In a study of suicide rates in Cook County, Illinois, Maris (1967) found the following frequencies (per 100,000 per year):

	White	Nonwhite
Upper Class	15.3	15.0
Middle Class	22.4	14.4
Lower Class	35.7	22.3

Clearly, these results partly oppose what Henry and Short predict. The suicide rate is highest for the group that is under the greatest external constraint, the lower class. Because other people often wield power over members of the lower class and they therefore tend to attribute responsibility to others, Henry and Short predicted that they would tend to commit less suicide and more homicide. But Maris' data indicate otherwise, showing that those in the lower classes direct aggression toward themselves more often than do members of the upper class.

Differences in suicidal and homicidal behavior between whites and blacks are in accord with the predictions made by Henry and Short. African Americans, who on average have much less social freedom than whites, have a lower suicide rate than whites and a higher murder rate. This same difference was noted in South Africa before the white government was replaced by a biracial government (Lester, 1989).

In a study stimulated by Henry and Short's theory, Littunen and Gaier (1963) compared suicide and homicide rates in Finland and the United States. Previous studies suggested that most Americans conform to peer group pressure, while those who live in Finland conform more to their own personal beliefs. In Henry and Short's terms, Americans have greater external restraints than Finns. The prediction that the suicide/homicide ratio would be lower in the United States than in Finland was confirmed. In 1957, the ratio was 2:1 in the U.S. and 10:1 in Finland.

Lester's (1986) research on the association between the quality of life and rates of suicide and homicide also confirms Henry and Short's theory. In nations where the quality of life is higher and where there are presumably fewer external restraints on behavior, the suicide rate is higher and the murder rate is lower. In the same way, in nations where the quality of life is poor and where there are many external sources of blame for misery (e.g., famine, civil war, totalitarian governments), the suicide rate is lower and the murder rate higher.

Although the basic assumption of Henry and Short's theory — that suicide is inward-directed aggression — has never been supported by empirical evidence, in many cases it appears that the theory can be used to generate correct predictions. However, many of the details of the theory may not be correct. For example, it is possible that external restraints act directly on adults to cause differences the ratio of suicide to homicide, in which case there would be no need to theorize about child-rearing practices as a determining factor.

SUMMARY

Studies on the relation between suicide and homicide rates among large groups of people have given inconsistent results, probably because the association between the two acts is too complex. The phenomenon of murder-suicides may yield some information on the relation between the two acts, but, again, the analysis of these acts seems to give different results, depending on the country being examined. In studies of Americans, the presence of guilt seems to be an important reason that suicide follows murder. In other countries, the significant elements of suicide after murder seem to be despair and a desire to be reunited with the victim in the afterlife. In some cases, suicidally inclined people who want to die but who do not want to take their own lives, may provoke another individual to murder them.

Because the acts of homicide and suicide are comparable in a number of ways, it is useful to determine why some people become murderers and others become suicides. One important theory, which is supported by some research, suggests that people who murder have experienced physical punishment and external constraints, and that suicides have been psychologically punished and have had fewer external constraints.

REFERENCES

Dorpat, T.L. Suicide in murderers. *Psychiatric Digest* 27(June): 51-55, 1986.

Halbwachs, M. *Les Causes du Suicide*. Paris: Felix Alcan, 1930.

Henry, A.F., and Short, J.F. *Suicide and Homicide*. Glencoe, IL: The Free Press, 1954.

Lester, D. Suicide, homicide and the quality of life. *Suicide and Life-Threatening Behavior* 16:389-392, 1986.

Lester, D. Personal violence (suicide and homicide) in South Africa. *Acta Psychiatrica Scandinavica* 79:235-237, 1989.

Lester, D. *Patterns of Suicide and Homicide in America*. Commack, NY: Nova Science Publishers, 1994.

Lester, D. *Patterns of Suicide and Homicide Around the World*. Commack, NY: Nova Science Publishers, 1995.

Littunen, Y. and Gaier, E.L. Social control and social integration. *International Journal of Social Psychiatry* 9: 165-173, 1963.

Maris, R. Suicide, status and mobility in Chicago. *Social Forces* 46:246-256, 1967.

Mowrer, O.H. *Learning Theory and the Symbolic Process*. New York: Wiley, 1968.

Pokorny, A.D. Human violence. *Journal of Criminal Law, Criminology and Police Science* 56:488-497, 1968.

Resnick, P.J. Child murder by parents. *American Journal of Psychiatry* 126:325-334, 1969.

West, D.J. *Murder Followed by Suicide*. Cambridge, MA: Harvard University Press, 1966.

Wolfgang, M.E. An analysis of homicide-suicide. *Journal of Clinical and Experimental Psychopathology* 19:208-217, 1957.

Wolfgang, M.E. Husband-wife homicides. *Journal of Social Therapy*

   2:263-271, 1958.
Wolfgang, M.E. Suicide by means of victim-precipitated homicide.
   Journal of Clinical and Experimental Psychopathology 20:335-349,
   1959.

9

The Social Context of Suicide

Suicide inevitably occurs within a social context. Although many suicidal people may feel that they are all alone in the world, they are not. Even if they don't have any friends, they have parents or parent-substitutes; they have worked together with others; they have had teachers and classmates; and they may have children of their own. The presence and nature of these social relationships and the extent to which society approves of them may have a great deal to do with the tendency to turn to suicidal behavior.

MARITAL STATUS AND SUICIDAL BEHAVIOR

The incidence of completed suicide seems to be lowest among married people. It is higher in the widowed and highest of all in divorced persons (Dublin, 1963; Smith et al., 1988). This holds true for most nations, for both men and women and for people of all ages, except perhaps adolescents.

There are, however, some interesting gender differences involving marriage. Gove (1972, 1979) noted that married women more often have psychiatric illness than married men. In contrast, never-married men have higher rates of psychiatric illness than never-married women. Gove concluded that marriage reduces psychiatric stress for men, but increases it for women and that marriage is more advantageous for men than for women. Gove extended his analyses to suicide and found that the ratio of suicide rates for the never-married and married was higher for men than for women. Although for both genders the never-married had the higher suicide rates, single men were 97 percent more likely to complete suicide than married men, whereas single women were only 47 percent more likely to complete suicide than married women.

In widowed persons, the death of the spouse seems to act as a precipitating factor in bringing about suicide. For the first four years of widowhood, the number of deaths from suicide exceeds the number due to all other causes (MacMahon and Pugh, 1965). Among people who have any tendency to regard suicide as a solution to their problems, the despair, loneliness and hopelessness of widowhood may encourage their suicidal preoccupation. If they have defined the spouse as the only person who was a source of nurturance and help, the bereaved may feel that they have no one to turn to. This may be objectively untrue; there may be many relatives and friends anxious to succor the bereaved, but as long as they feel subjectively alone, they may perceive suicide as the only escape from their misery. And there is also the possibility that people who had few social contacts may objectively be isolated after the death of a spouse. In either case, fantasies of joining the spouse in an afterlife, as well as the need to escape the pain of bereavement, may lead to suicide.

In divorced persons, the high incidence of suicide has a more complicated background. As with widows or widowers, divorced people have lost an important source of nurturance. However, the divorced differ from the widowed in that for the former, the loss was brought about, at least in part, by their own doing. The suicides of divorced people may be, in part, a self-inflicted punishment for the self-produced loss of their spouse. Some investigators of this issue have suggested that divorced people, having suffered a loss as a result of turning their aggression toward the spouse (by means of the divorce itself), may then turn their anger inward and, in extreme cases, kill themselves (Henry and Short, 1954). Another possibility is that both the divorce and the later suicide stem from some profound unhappiness with the world, and that both are attempts to resolve this condition. It may be that during marriage, individuals were able to place all the blame for their general unhappiness on their spouses. After the divorce has occurred and they find that they are still unhappy, suicide may be seen as the only possible escape.

THE MARITAL RELATIONSHIP AND SUICIDE

Although the suicide rate is relatively low for married people, marriage does not confer any magic immunity from self-destruction. The occurrence of suicide among married people provides an opportunity to look at ongoing social relationships as they influence the tendency to suicide. An important aspect of the marital relationship seems to be found in the differences between the suicidal spouses and the nonsuicidal partners, especially as far as self-images are concerned (Hattem, 1964). The ways in which suicidal and nonsuicidal spouses perceive their own personalities seem to be almost diametrically opposed. Suicidal partners tend to see themselves as self-effacing and masochistic, whereas nonsuicidal spouses see themselves as competitive and narcissistic. These opposing self-images fit well together; the suicidal partner has an excellent chance to be self-effacing while the nonsuicidal partner is overbearing and competitive, and the tendency of the nonsuicidal partner to seek only his own satisfaction is encouraged by the need of the suicidal spouse to have her desires ignored. In spite of the meshing needs that exist between the partners, the suicidal spouse often blames his suicidal behavior on his spouse's rejection.

Married people who make frequent, low-risk suicidal gestures may have special problems within the marital relationship. For example, the spouses may communicate more often in a manner known as double-binding, in which several mutually contradictory messages come across at the same time. A wife may wear provocative clothing and behave seductively, but become angry and criticize her husband when he approaches her sexually. The double-binding person responds poorly to his spouse's attempt to clarify the contradictory messages and denies that there is any problem. The spouses of such people may use suicidal behavior to interrupt and change the kinds of communications that are coming from the double-binder.

Marriages that have a suicidal partner are marked by poor communication and the presence of destructive conflicts such as quarreling, heavy alcohol use and infidelity (Lester, 1992). In general, the suicidal partner is the more psychologically disturbed of the two.

It has been long thought that the presence of children reduces the risk of suicide (Durkheim, 1897; Dublin and Bunzel, 1933), and recent research supports this assumption (Hoyer and Lund, 1993). The presence of children may provide more reasons to go on living and may increase the social ties that bind people to one another, suggesting a greater stability in the marriage.

GENERAL SOCIAL RELATIONS AND SUICIDE

The problems of social adjustment that are reflected in the marriages and divorces of suicidal persons are characteristic of their relations not only with their marital partners, but also with people in general. People who are at high risk for suicide tend to have been unable to maintain warm, mutual relationships throughout their lives. They do not seem able to express their need to be dependent and receive help from others, in spite of the fact that their dependency needs are perhaps more urgent than those of nonsuicidal people. The result of this inability to express powerful needs is, of course, that the needs remain unsatisfied. The lack of gratification is intensified by the fact that even when others go out of their way to be supportive, suicidal people tend to retreat or to deny that any help is being offered.

Perhaps because of their inability to express dependency needs, suicidal people often feel socially isolated to a greater extent than do nonsuicidal persons. There is also a tendency for suicidal individuals to lack hope that their life will improve and that they will no longer be social isolates. Suicidal people tend to believe that the people with whom they have close relationships feel negatively about them. At the same time, their feelings about their companions are much more ambivalent than the feelings of nonsuicidal people.

Perhaps this expectation of negative feelings from other people, and their ambivalent feelings toward others, is based on the suicidal person's lack of confidence in his ability to handle other people. A number of strategies are available to all of us in our attempts to get what we want from other people. Ganzler (1964) labeled some of these strategies:

- mature-corrective (such as discussing the issue)

- positive-manipulative and diplomatic (being affectionate)

- distance-producing or avoiding-repressive (staying aloof)

- managerial-autocratic and belittling (being bossy)

- third-party strategies (making the other person jealous)

- emotional responses and negative feeling (getting angry)

Suicidal persons have been found to express little confidence in any of the above-listed strategies for controlling interpersonal relations. In particular, they show the least confidence in the first two strategies, the very ones that are most likely to bring about a lasting solution to interpersonal problems.

SOCIAL RELATIONSHIPS AND
THE SUICIDAL ADOLESCENT

The feeling of social helplessness, which is characteristic of suicidal persons in general, is particularly strong in the suicidal adolescent. Adolescence, especially in American and European cultures, is a time of special stress. Adolescents must break away from their intense childhood involvement with their parents, brothers and sisters and find a place for themselves within the larger society. This is a difficult task at best, and it may be rendered still more difficult by the fact that parents may resent and oppose the "loss" of their children. Even for the nonsuicidal adolescent, bewilderment about how to deal with interpersonal relations is a common emotion during adolescence.

In many countries, adolescence is increasingly becoming a time of risk for suicide. While the people who are personally associated with the suicidal individual are most concerned, adolescent suicide is a subject that most everyone is very worried about. One reason for this concern is that most adults remember how difficult their own adolescent years were and they feel sympathy when they hear about young people wanting to die, or actually dying, as a result of their difficulties. In addition, the fact that adolescent suicide occurs at a time when the victim is still dependent on his parents may lead parents to feel that they are responsible, at least in part, for the death of their own child. There is also a general attitude that it is tragic for people to die "before they have had a chance to live." Older suicides, though their acts cause grief and consternation among those close to them, may be perceived as at least having tasted life before deciding in favor of death; adolescents are considered to be too inexperienced to make such a decision. There are many reasons that we all have special concern about suicidal behavior in adolescents, and this concern has generated a good deal of research.

One approach to the study of adolescent suicide has been to look at the kinds of experiences that suicidal teenagers have had since early childhood (Jacobs, 1971). In general, it is unusually common for them to have a history of difficulties in the decade preceding adolescence, several changes of residence, hospitalizations, and other disruptive events. Divorces followed by quick remarriages of the custodial parents — marriages that also tend to be unstable — are also common. For the suicidal adolescent, once adolescence begins, problems increase even beyond the multiplying difficulties faced by the average teenager. Immediately before their attempt, suicidal adolescents often experience further disruptions, particularly the kinds that dissolve meaningful relationships, especially romances. The suicide attempt very rarely occurs without warning to others; in fact it is foreshadowed by an escalation of problems between the parents and the child, resulting in still more loss of human contact for the child. Often the child responds to the original difficulties in a nonconfrontational way, such as by running away from home. The parents respond in negative ways to this attempt to handle problems and tend to be punitive; they nag, yell and use physical discipline, sometimes to an unusually great extent. The culmination of this increased alienation within the family is that adolescents feel that they have exhausted all possible solutions to the problem and attempt suicide.

Research has also explored how suicidal adolescents regard their own social relationships. Considerable differences exist between the feelings of suicidal and nonsuicidal adolescents toward their friends and relatives. Nonsuicidal adolescents generally feel that there are people in their lives to whom they can turn for help. There are also people that they dislike and resent. For the nonsuicidal adolescent, these two categories rarely overlap: if people are resented, they are not thought of as a source of help, and if they are a source of help, they are not resented. For suicidal adolescents, these two views of other people are confused. There may be great resentment against a person who is seen as a source of help. At the same time, suicidal adolescents tend to resent their parents more than do their nonsuicidal peers (Lester, 1969).

Suicidal adolescents typically feel alienated from others, and they often harbor a great deal of resentment toward the world. Repeated threats of suicide, combined with a history of aggressive and antisocial behavior, which is common in the background of suicidal adolescents (Pfeffer et al., 1980), tend to elicit rejecting behavior from friends and relatives. Although the friends and relatives of suicidal adolescents may feel pity and compassion for them at some level, they may also harbor strong feelings of anger and resentment. (Remember also that the parents of suicidal adolescents are frequently troubled with psychological problems, including depression, alcohol abuse and violent tendencies. Moreover, physical and sexual abuse is not uncommon in the lives of suicidal adolescents.) Communication of parental anger may be inhibited by guilt over having such feelings, in which case, it may be communicated unconsciously. Parents have been known to encourage their children to commit suicide. As the problems between adolescents and their families escalate, the affectionate feelings of those close to the adolescent become less and less easy to arouse, and negative feelings become even stronger. Thus suicidal behavior may make other people feel and act in a rejecting way, which may confirm to suicidal adolescents that they are right to resent the world. The same process may also reinforce feelings that they are not worth caring about.

SUICIDE AND THE EXPERIENCE OF LOSS

So far in this chapter we have looked primarily at the kinds of social relationships that are present in people's lives at the time they display suicidal tendencies. Another important question involves the kinds of relationships they have had in the past and the extent to which they have suffered disruption or loss of important relationships. Other losses, as of a job or of some physical ability, may also be important in the development of suicidal behavior; for example, research indicates that suicide is much more common in those who are unemployed (Platt, 1984). Among suicidal women, loss of a personal relationship is still a common factor, though changing sex roles are making this gender difference less pronounced (Canetto, 1992-93). (Many publicized cases in the U.S. and Europe seem to indicate that men are more likely than women to respond to the breakup of an interpersonal relationship by murdering their ex-lover before committing suicide.)

It is clear that most people experience severe loss without becoming suicidal. What is the process that leads a person from loss to suicide? It may be based on changes in self-directed attitudes. To a considerable extent, people's attitudes toward themselves are based on their estimates of how other people feel about them. Our own judgment of ourselves has much to do with the way we are reflected in the mirror of other people's opinions. Many losses, whether of people, situations or things, may realistically imply a rather ugly image in that mirror. Loss of a job or a lover may mean that life will be more difficult and lonely for a while, but it also means that other people have made some highly negative judgments. People can respond to those negative judgments in several ways: they can change their behavior, they can decide that the disapproving person is wrong, or they can change their opinion of themselves in a negative direction. If they take the last option, they may lose confidence in themselves, communicate the lack of confidence to others, and receive further rejection. The spiral may end with the conviction that there is no alternative except suicide.

SUMMARY

From the examples in this chapter, we can see that poor social integration contributes to suicidal tendencies. Suicide is far more likely for socially isolated people who have unsatisfactory, ambivalent relationships and for those whose closest relationships are permeated with resentment. Suicide seems to be higher among those who are widowed and higher still among those who are divorced than it is among married people (even though there are differences between men and women). People who are at high risk for suicide are often unable to express their need to be dependent and receive help from others, despite the fact that their dependency needs are often more urgent than nonsuicidal people. We can learn a lot about the role of social relationships in suicide by looking at the situation of suicidal adolescents. The teenage years are a period of time in which difficult adjustments to new kinds of social relationships must be made. Finally, for people of all ages, the loss of a close relationship, whether by accident or by deliberate withdrawal, may play an important role in the development of suicidal behavior. The experience of a hard loss, whether it is the loss of an important relationship or the loss of a job, may precipitate suicidal behavior. Suicidal behavior does not occur without warning, and one of the most telling warning signs can be found in the quality of an individual's social relationships.

REFERENCES

Canetto, S.S. She died for love and he for glory. *Omega* 26:1-17, 1992-93.

Dublin, L. *Suicide*. New York: Ronald Press, 1963.

Dublin, L. and Bunzel, B. *To Be or Not to Be*. New York: Harrison Smith and Robert Haas, 1933.

Durkheim, E. *Le Suicide*. Paris: Felix Alcan, 1897.

Ganzler, S. Some interpersonal and social dimensions of suicidal behavior. *Dissertation Abstracts* 28B:1192-1193, 1964.

Gove, W. Sex, marital status and suicide. *Journal of Health and Social Behavior* 13:204-213, 1972.

Gove, W. Sex differences in the epidemiology of mental disorder. In E.S. Gomberg and V. Franks (eds.), *Gender and Disordered Behavior*. New York: Brunner/Mazel, 1979.

Hattem, J.V. Precipitating role of discordant interpersonal relationships in suicidal behavior. *Dissertation Abstracts* 25:1335-1336, 1964.

Henry, A.F. and Short, J.F. *Suicide and Homicide*. Glencoe, IL: The Free Press, 1954.

Hoyer, G. and Lund, E. Suicide among women related to number of children in marriage. *Archives of General Psychiatry* 50:134-137, 1993.

Jacobs, J. *Adolescent Suicide*. New York: Wiley, 1971.

Lester, D. Resentment and dependency in the suicidal individual. *Journal of General Psychology* 81:137-145, 1969.

Lester, D. *Why People Kill Themselves*. Springfield, IL: Charles C Thomas, 1992.

MacMahon, B. and Pugh, T. Suicide in the widowed. *American Journal of Epidemiology* 81:23-31, 1965.

Pfeffer, C., Conte, H., Plutchik, R. and Jerrett, I. Suicidal behavior in latency-age children. *Journal of the American Academy of Child Psychiatry* 19:703-710, 1980.

Platt, S.D. Unemployment and suicidal behavior. *Social Science and Medicine* 19:93-115, 1984.

Smith, J.C., Mercy, J.A. and Conn, J.M. Marital status and the risk of suicide. *American Journal of Public Health* 78:78-80, 1988.

10

Suicidal Communications and the Suicide Note

For some people, a suicide attempt can be a way — a very severe way — of communicating that they are extremely unhappy. Many suicidologists argue that the communicative motive of attempts is more important than the death-seeking motive. Farberow and Shneidman, for example, called their book on attempted suicide *The Cry for Help*. I do not mean to imply that completed suicides do not have communicative goals; although these people will not be around to see the effects of their suicides, the motivation to kill themselves may very well include the feeling that they will benefit because they were able to communicate their feelings, to let other people know how they felt. Of course, if they believe in life after death, they may expect to be able to "witness" the effects of their suicide on others.

Obviously, there are many ways other than suicide to communicate feelings; the communication channels of suicidal individuals must be woefully inadequate if they feel compelled to communicate though suicide. Often they cannot communicate well because their relationships with other people are so troubled (see Chapter 9).

In this chapter, we will look at the attempts people make to use less desperate forms of communication prior to a suicidal act. As discussed previously, the suicidal act is usually preceded by many behavioral changes, and attempts to communicate distress are one of these changes.

HOW FREQUENT ARE PRE-SUICIDAL COMMUNICATIONS?

One group of researchers (Robins et al., 1959) interviewed the relatives of a sample of completed suicides in order to find out how and to what extent the suicidal intent had been communicated prior to the actual act. They found only one kind of nonverbal communication — a nonfatal suicide attempt — but 26 kinds of verbal communication that ranged from bold statements of suicidal intent, to mentioning other people's suicides, to calling up old friends. Some 69 percent of the suicides in the sample had communicated their intent, with the average number of communications per person estimated at about 3.2. Most of the communications had taken place within one year before the suicide. Of the people who had made longstanding suicidal communications, a number had intensified their efforts during the year of the suicide. These communications had been made to a wide variety of friends and relatives. A more subtle cue was when the person visited a physician in the weeks prior to his suicide, though he did not necessarily bring up the topic of suicide (Hawton and Blackstock, 1976). Perhaps these people really wanted to tell the doctor about their problems, but were unable to discuss them when they finally had the opportunity.

More recent studies have reported that 94 percent of completed suicides (Wrobleski and McIntosh, 1986) and 92 percent of suicide attempters (Wolk-Wasserman, 1986) made at least one communication attempt prior to the act. Beck and Lester (1976) found that the critical decision for completed suicides was whether to communicate or not, while the critical decision for suicide attempters was whether to communicate before or after the attempt.

REACTIONS OF OTHERS TO COMMUNICATIONS

Studies show that the reactions of friends and relatives to a suicidal communication vary. In some cases (for example, if the suicidal person is a chronic alcoholic), the reaction may often be skeptical, especially because the person may have been threateniing suicide for years. If suicidal individuals tend to make unrealistic statements on other topics, their friends and family may take seriously their very serious suicidal statements. In Robins' study, most of the people who received a suicidal communication said it made them feel anxious and helpless. Even though they felt distressed, they did not feel capable of preventing the suicide or of turning over responsibility to someone else. They often discounted the communications, citing the familiar myth that "those who talk about suicide don't do it." The recipients often convinced themselves that the person's suicidal mood was only temporary.

We should also take into account that recipients of suicidal communications are often personally involved with the suicidal individual and, therefore, they may be a factor that contributes to the person's suicidal crisis. Indeed, in some cases, personally related recipients may harbor strong resentment toward the suicidal person and may actually wish him dead. Therefore, to serve their own desires, they may choose to ignore or "not notice" the suicidal communication.

WHY DO PEOPLE COMMUNICATE SUICIDAL FEELINGS?

What motivations lead people to communicate their feelings to other people prior to a suicidal act? The reason depends partly on the suicidal individual. After their interviews with the relatives and friends of suicides, Robins' group came up with four possibilities:

1. Some suicidal people are ambivalent about dying and their suicidal behavior is a "cry for help." If we consider the suicidal act itself as a form of communication, we might say that these people try more and more desperate methods of communication until they die in their attempt to be understood. In any case, we must assume that people who make suicidal statements are not always wholly bent on dying, for they are giving other people a chance to prevent their suicides.

2. Potential suicides may want to prepare the people in their lives in order to reduce the shock they will feel when they find out about their death. We would expect this motive to exist primarily among people who want to die so they can escape a life of suffering. The desire to prepare significant others does not, however, seem congruent with the resentment and manipulativeness that are often characteristic of suicidal people.

3. Some suicidal individuals have no desire to die but simply wish to threaten and taunt other people with the possibility of their suicide. As noted above, most people are severely threatened and helpless when they hear statements of suicidal intent and if this reaction is the suicidal person's goal, then he usually gets what he wants. Why would people go on to commit suicide, then, if threats are so effective? There could be many reasons. Family and friends, although initially agitated by suicide threats, may eventually begin to ignore them. Or, even if the recipient remains distressed about the possibility of the individual's suicide, the suicidal individual may become dissatisfied with the way his threats are affecting the recipient. Another possibility is that because suicide is usually deter-

mined by a complex of motives, another issue — for example, guilt about their behavior — when combined with the previous motivation of hurting others, might be enough to trigger suicide.

4. Some people may not really intend their suicidal statements as communication. They may be preoccupied with thoughts about death and their remarks may be a reflection of their preoccupation rather than an attempt to communicate. However, certain remarks ("You'll be sorry when you find me hanging in the shower stall!") clearly cannot be attributed to preoccupation.

THE SUICIDE NOTE

The one kind of pre-suicidal communication that has gained fame through novels and films is the suicide note. This communication, generally written shortly before the suicidal act occurs, is of great practical value to suicidologists. The suicide note is one of the few pieces of objective evidence available for study after a suicide has been completed. When researchers interview family and friends, the information they get is often distorted by the informant's memory, if not deliberately altered or censored. Even the suicide's medical or psychiatric history, if it is available, may misrepresent the suicidal person. The suicide note alone opens a window onto the writer's thinking just before his death.

Do most suicides leave suicide notes? The practice is actually not as widespread as is commonly thought. In a thorough study of suicide in Los Angeles County, Shneidman and Farberow (1961) found that 35 percent of male and 39 percent of female completed suicides left notes that were found by the authorities. About 30 percent of these left more than one note, directing separate notes to different people. In cases of attempted suicide, only 2 percent of the males and 1 percent of the females left notes that were found. These figures are undoubtedly underestimates of the true number of those who write notes. Attempters could easily destroy the note before it was found, and friends or family of completed suicides might be reluctant to report that a note was found.

Faked vs. Genuine Notes

It is very important to be able to determine whether a suicide note is the real thing or a fake. People fake or tamper with suicide notes for various reasons. When a murderer wants the murder he committed to look like a suicide, he might write a suicide note supposedly written by the person he actually killed. Also, people might write a suicide note because they want it to *look* like they have killed themselves when, in fact, they have changed their identity. This actually happened, as Seiden and Tauber found out, when in 1970 they collected the suicide notes allegedly written by people who allegedly jumped off the Golden Gate Bridge in San Francisco. It turned out that none of these people had committed suicide; they wanted to start new lives with new identities.

The ability to correctly determine whether or not a suicide note is genuine depends in large part on the evaluator's experience with suicide cases and specifically with suicide notes. According to Osgood and Walker (1959), graduate students who had no experience with suicide notes did no better than chance when trying to tell which of a pair of notes was genuine: out of 33 pairs of genuine and faked notes, the graduate students made an average of 16.5 correct choices. The evaluators who had experience with suicide notes chose correctly on an average of 28.5 of the pairs. Recently, Lester (1994) found that suicidologists could distinguish genuine from fake suicide notes but were unable to distinguish whether the genuine notes were written by completed suicides or attempted suicides, perhaps suggesting that the motives of completed and attempted suicides may be similar.

In another study (Frederick, 1968), genuine suicide notes were recopied by hand by nonsuicidal people. A group consisting of graphologists, secretaries and detectives was then asked to judge, on the basis of the handwriting, which notes had been written by suicides. The detectives and secretaries performed at chance level, but the graphologists were able to identify the genuine notes quite accurately.

Content Analysis of the Suicide Note

It may be possible to develop a means of analyzing the ideas contained in notes and the way they are expressed. Suicidologists have analyzed suicide notes in terms of the motives implied in them, the emotion that predominates and their syntactical qualities. There have also been analyses based on the predictions of particular theories. Here we will discuss some of the analyses that have been conducted and their results.

Jacobs (1967) has taken the point of view that the actual performance of a suicidal act is not possible until suicidal individuals have broken through the cultural constraints that exist concerning the behavior of suicide. A suicide note may reflect the intellectual

and emotional mechanisms the person used to overcome his culturally determined bias against suicide. To overcome the constraints,
individuals must be in a situation in which they:

- are faced with extremely distressing problems

- view their current situation as being part of a long history of
  similar crises

- believe that death is the only solution to their problems

- become so isolated socially that they cannot share their distress
  with others

- overcome their belief that suicide is irrational or immoral

- succeed in this thinking because their social isolation makes
  them feel less constrained by societal rules

- rationalize in such a way that they can see the problem as not
  of their own making and that they have no other solution

- make provisions so that their problems will not continue when
  they are dead

Precautions to assure that troubles will not occur after death can
take several forms. If suicidal individuals are religious, they may
become atheists and thus avoid questions of divine punishment. On
the other hand, they may seek reassurance that God can forgive
anything, even suicide; in their suicide note, they may ask God's
forgiveness and request that others pray for their soul. Or they may
develop a belief in reincarnation while overlooking the possible
negative consequences of the doctrine of Karma.

Jacobs used four categories of suicide notes that he based on elements from the list above. The first category contains most of the
aspects described in the list. These writers beg forgiveness, maintain
that their problems are not of their own making, affirm that the
problems have become intolerable, decide that death is a necessity,
and finally communicate that they know what they are doing, but
realize that readers of their note probably will not understand them.
An example of this kind of note follows (Jacobs, 1967, pp. 67-68):

It is hard to say why you don't want to live. I have only one
real reason. The three people I have in the world which I love
don't love me.

Tom, I love you so dearly but you have told me you don't

want me and you don't love me. I never thought you would let me go this far, but I am now at the end which is the best thing for you. You have so many problems and I am sorry I added to them.

Daddy, I hurt you so much and I guess I really hurt myself. You only wanted the very best for me and you must believe this is it.

Mommy, you tried so hard to make me happy and to make things right for all of us. I love you too so very much. You did not fail. I did. I have no place to go so I am back where I always seem to find peace. I have failed in everything I have done and I hope I do not fail in this. I love you all dearly and am sorry this is the way I have to say goodbye.

Please forgive me and be happy. Your wife and your daughter.

In Jacob's second category of suicide note, writers have an incurable or painful illness. They are less likely to ask for forgiveness or indulgence because they feel that readers will be sympathetic. The reality of the illness makes it unnecessary for the writers to be as thorough in their rationalizations as other suicides would be.

In the third category of notes, writers do not ask for forgiveness or give the usual reasons for the suicide. Instead, they blame their suicide on other people. These notes are usually quite brief, as in this example (Jacobs, 1967, p. 69):

Mary, I hope you're satisfied, Bill

The fourth category is the instructional note that amounts to a "last will and testament." These notes are very impersonal and do not explain the reasons for the act. Jacobs reported that of 112 suicide notes he examined, only 10 did not fit into one of these four categories.

Leenaars (1991) analyzed theories of suicide for the essential components of the suicidal state and reduced these components to 100 basic elements. When he examined suicide notes for the presence or absence of these elements, he identified eight commonly found clusters of elements:

1. *Unbearable psychological pain.* Suicidal individuals are in great psychological pain and feel hopeless and helpless about all efforts to reduce this pain.

2. *Interpersonal relations.* Suicidal individuals are usually experi-

encing difficulties in their interpersonal relationships, and
their basic needs are not being met by these relationships.

3. *Rejection-aggression.* Some suicidal individuals seem to turn
inward and onto themselves the anger that they originally felt
toward others.

4. *Inability to adjust.* Suicidal individuals often perceive themselves as unable to make the adjustments that their situation
seems to demand.

5. *Indirect expressions.* Suicide notes often contain confusing, contradictory messages and evidence of unconscious motives.

6. *Identification-egression.* Suicidal individuals often show an
intense attachment to a lost or rejecting person (or perhaps an
ideal) and cannot bear the pain of the loss.

7. *Ego.* Suicidal individuals lack the ability to develop constructive tendencies needed to overcome their situation.

8. *Cognitive constriction.* Suicidal individuals tend to think rigidly,
have a narrow focus and tunnel vision, making it difficult for
them to find alternative solutions.

Interestingly, in their studies, Leenaars and his associates (1988)
found almost no difference, whether or not these themes were present, in the suicide notes of men and women or in the suicide notes
of completed suicides and attempted suicides (Leenaars et al., 1992).
However, when Leenaars studied the suicide notes of elderly people, he found fewer indirect expressions and fewer problems with
interpersonal relations (Leenaars, 1994).

A number of research studies have compared genuine suicide
notes with simulated suicide notes written by nonsuicidal people at
the request of the researcher. Shneidman and Farberow (1957)
found that the genuine notes contained more intense feelings of
hatred, vengeance and self-blame. They also found that the genuine
notes contained more neutral statements (i.e., showing neither positive nor negative feelings), but this was probably a result of the
greater number of instructions in the genuine notes.

Spiegel and Neuringer (1963) found evidence that writers of genuine suicide notes made an effort to overcome the fear and dread
that are usually aroused when one's own death is contemplated.
The genuine note-writers they surveyed reduced their fear and
dread by avoiding the direct mention of suicide in the notes and by
not being explicit. (One might ask, however, why people who are

deceiving themselves about their imminent suicide should write suicide notes at all.)

Finally, Osgood and Walker (1959) found that the writers of the genuine notes they studied more often used the same words and phrases over and over again, and they used more inclusive terms such as "always" and "never." Osgood and Walker saw these tendencies as signs of stereotypy and dichotomous thinking. These kinds of tendencies appear in times of intense stress, and thinking in black and white terms may make the writers feel that suicide is the only alternative: either their life must be perfect or they must die.

SUMMARY

People may attempt suicide or even complete suicide as a desperate effort to communicate their feelings of unhappiness and their desire to die. Such acts are almost invariably preceded by less severe methods of communicating. People communicate their suicidal desires for various reasons; most often they are crying for help, but sometimes they want to prepare loved ones for their eventual suicide or they want to frighten or threaten others with the possibility that they will kill themselves. Unfortunately, the seriousness of pre-suicidal communications is often discounted by friends and relatives. Completed suicides are commonly preceded by a last communicative act — the writing of a suicide note. Suicide notes can offer investigators a good deal of important information about the individual who writes (or wrote) them. Studies have shown that suicide notes written by different people are often quite similar. They commonly mention psychological pain, problems with specific people, as well as rationalizations and requests for forgiveness for the suicidal action.

REFERENCES

Beck, A.T. and Lester, D. Components of suicidal intent in completed and attempted suicide. *Journal of Psychology* 92:35-38, 1976.

Farberow, N.L. and Shneidman, E.S. *The Cry for Help.* New York: McGraw-Hill, 1961.

Frederick, C.J. An investigation of handwriting of suicidal persons through suicide notes. *Journal of Abnormal Psychology* 73:263-267, 1968.

Hawton, K. and Blackstock, E. General practice aspects of self-poisoning and self-injury. *Psychological Medicine* 6:571-575, 1976.

Jacobs, J. A phenomenological study of suicide notes. *Social Problems* 15:60-72, 1967.

Leenaars, A.A. Are women's suicides really different from men's? *Women and Health* 18:17-33, 1988.

Leenaars, A.A. Suicide notes and their implications for intervention. *Crisis* 12(1):1-20, 1991.

Leenaars, A.A. Suicide across the life span with particular reference to the elderly. In D. Lester and M. Tallmer (eds.), *Now I Lay Me Down: Suicide in the Elderly*. Philadelphia: The Charles Press, 1994.

Leenaars, A.A., Lester, D., Wenckstern, S., et al. Comparison of suicide notes and parasuicide notes. *Death Studies* 16:331-342, 1992.

Lester, D. Can suicidologists distinguish between suicide notes from completers and attempters? *Perceptual and Motor Skills* 79:1498, 1994.

Osgood, C. and Walker, E.G. Motivation and language behavior. *Journal of Abnormal and Social Psychology* 59:58-67, 1959.

Robins, E., Gassner, S., Kayes, J., et al. The communication of suicidal intent. *American Journal of Psychiatry* 115:724-733, 1959.

Seiden, R and Tauber, R. Pseudocides versus suicides. In *Proceedings of the 5th International Congress for Suicide Prevention*. Vienna: International Association for Suicide Prevention, 1970.

Shneidman, E.S. and Farberow, N.L. Some comparisons between genuine and simulated suicide notes in terms of Mowrer's concepts of discomfort and relief. *Journal of General Psychology* 56:251-256, 1957.

Shneidman, E.S. and Farberow, N.L. Statistical comparisons between committed and attempted suicides. In N.L. Farberow and E.S. Shneidman (eds.), *The Cry for Help*. New York: McGraw-Hill, 1961.

Spiegel, D.E. and Neuringer, C. Role of dread in suicidal behavior. *Journal of Abnormal and Social Psychology* 66:507-511, 1963.

Wolk-Wasserman, D. Suicidal communications of persons attempting suicide and response of significant others. *Acta Psychiatrica Scandinavica* 73:481-499, 1986.

Wrobleski, A. and McIntosh, J.L. Clues to suicide and suicide survivors. In R. Cohen-Sandler (ed.), *Proceedings of the 19th Annual Meeting*. Denver: American Association of Suicidology, 1986.

11

How the Suicidal Person Thinks

As people go through life, their choice of behavior may depend in part on the nature and quality of their thought processes. Some people make poor choices because they do not use logic when they try to solve their problems. Sometimes the problem is that they are not good at forming a logical conclusion, but more often their trouble is due to the fact that they distort the premises — in other words, their initial perceptions of something are skewed, thereby corrupting the conclusions they reach. Consider the following syllogism:

Some hippies are atheists.

Some atheists are anarchists.

Therefore some hippies may be anarchists.

To conclude that *all* hippies are anarchists would be an error in logic. If a person makes this sort of error in logic when he was deciding, for example, what he thought about what kind of person he was, he would not make out very well. A second and more common kind of error people make is to distort the meaning of words, thereby causing an error in the premises of otherwise logical sequences. For example, a person might distort the term "hippies" to mean all students or to mean all men with beards, or distort the term "anarchists" to mean "people who disagree with me politically." When a person makes these kinds of distortions, even a logically correct conclusion would have a totally incorrect meaning. This sort of distortion occurs more readily with material that is highly personal and emotionally loaded.

Suicidologists have made some studies of both these distortions of the thought process: illogical reasoning and distortion of the premises.

PARALOGIC

One type of logical error is often called paleologic or paralogic and is thought to be common in the deductive reasoning of schizophrenics. This type of error is shown in the following syllogistic reasoning:

All As are Bs.

All Cs are Bs.

Therefore, all As are Cs.

The person who makes this error assumes that there are no Bs other than As or Cs. Von Domarus, who originally described paralogic in 1944, gave this example of the type of flaw found in schizophrenic reasoning:

The Virgin Mary was a virgin.

I am a virgin.

Therefore, I am the Virgin Mary.

Shneidman and Farberow (1957) felt that although this kind of error in logic might indeed play a part in the reasoning of psychotic suicides, it is not generally found in other types of suicide; however, they did not present any cases to illustrate this.

DISTORTION OF IDEAS AND PREMISES

There are several ways in which the thinking of suicidal people can be distorted — other than the making of paralogical errors. Their thinking may be dichotomous; it may be rigid; or it may use terms ambiguously, although they use all other ideas correctly.

Dichotomous thinking involves the use of extreme value systems. It means thinking in terms of black and white, with no shades of gray. (This kind of thinking was discussed in connection with suicide notes in Chapter 10. Suicidal people may believe that there are only two possibilities for them: a perfect life or else death. We assume, of course, that dichotomous thinking would apply not only to the question of life and death, but to other decisions as well.)

Dichotomous evaluative thinking has been studied by Neuringer (1961, 1967), using the Semantic Differential Test. The Semantic Differential requires the respondent to rate abstract concepts (such as democracy, love and life) using scales such as good-bad, dirty-clean or happy-sad. The respondent may rate the concept as very bad, moderately bad, mildly bad, mildly good, moderately good, or very good.

Neuringer had his respondents rate a number of individual concepts that could be paired into opposites (such as life-death or honor-shame). If the ratings of opposites were mirror images of each other, the person was considered to be thinking dichotomously. (Life and death would have mirror-image ratings if life was rated as very good, very clean and very happy, while death was rated as very bad, very dirty and very sad.) Neuringer found that suicidal people exhibited the most extreme dichotomous thinking, normal people had the least and people who were emotionally disturbed but nonsuicidal fell in between.

Neuringer (1964) also looked at rigid thinking in suicidal people. His primary means of testing rigidity was by administering an attitude test called the California F-Scale. This test asks questions about an individual's political, religious and social opinions and is based on the idea that people who have unusually conservative opinions are rigid thinkers who are incapable of changing preconceived ideas even when they have new information. The F-Scale is known to be correlated with other measures of rigidity. For example, those who score high on the F-Scale also seem rigid on a reversible-figure test (such as a two-dimensional line drawing of a three-dimensional cube). Flexible observers see the reversal occur frequently, while those who are considered rigid report infrequent reversals.

Neuringer found that suicidal people scored high as rigid thinkers and that nonsuicidal emotionally disturbed people did not. It is possible that such rigid thinking could lead to suicide. Once rigid thinkers orient themselves toward suicidal behavior, once they react with severe distress to the circumstances of their lives, their ideas and feelings might be extremely difficult to change, regardless of how their lives might be improved as a result. This rigid quality of thinking can often be detected in suicide notes, where words such as "all" and "none" or "always" and "never" are frequently found. For example, a suicidal person may rigidly view a single, one-time behavior by a relative as an indication of how that person will always behave. Once the idea is present, no amount of different behavior is enough to alter their judgment. Indeed, rigidity of thinking may work together with other characteristics of suicidal people to produce a rigid picture of loved ones that is far from realistic.

Neuringer's work on the thinking processes of suicidal people has been applied in a study of German attempted suicides by Schmidtke and Schaller (1994). Because their subjects' thinking did not differ from nonsuicidal psychiatric patients, Schmidke and

Schaller concluded that the cognitive style of dichotomous evaluations and rigid thinking is characteristic of people who are in depressive states and in a crisis. Both of these groups differed from normal respondents. Schmidtke and Schaller did find evidence that attempted suicides react more impulsively to and in crisis situations.

DEFICIENCIES IN PROBLEM-SOLVING

In recent years, research has also examined the problem-solving skills of suicidal and nonsuicidal people, especially when they are confronted with interpersonal problems. Schotte and Clum (1987) found that suicidal patients were deficient in their ability to generate possible solutions for hypothetical interpersonal problems. They were also less likely to foresee the negative consequences of some of the solutions they chose. Based on this research, McLeavey, Daly, Ludgate and Murray (1994) trained one group of attempted suicides to improve their interpersonal problem-solving skills and found that these patients were much better at solving their subsequent interpersonal problems and were less likely to repeat their suicide attempts.

"Catalogic" is the name given by Shneidman and Farberow (1957) to an error that they consider to be frequent in suicidal thinking. Catalogic is the ambiguous use of a specific term, most commonly concerning the concept of "self." In particular, suicidal people confuse the self as they personally experience themselves with the self that is experienced by other people. The following argument is an example of catalogic:

> If anyone kills himself, he will get attention.
>
> I will kill myself.
>
> Therefore, I will get attention.

Shneidman and Farberow maintained that catalogic is a common error when considering one's own death, whether by suicide or otherwise. It may occur because people cannot imagine their own death, the cessation of any and all experience, a state in which the self as experienced by the self is no longer possible.

There could be several exceptions, Shneidman and Farberow noted, to the general idea of catalogic as the only error that could lead to suicide. Suicide would occur in the absence of catalogic if certain other unusual situations were present.

1. Some suicidal individuals actually want nothingness and nonexistence. Their suicidal intent may be based on the need to escape from pain — what Shneidman (1993) now calls "psychache." Shneidman and Farberow labeled these "surcease" suicides. Such people would not be making a catalogical error.

2. Some people believe that there is a life after death and that they will continue to experience the self. However, not all religious beliefs hold that the individual will be cognizant of events on earth after death. Even if a religious teaching does not recognize this state, catalogic could still occur.

3. Some persons may place their highest emphasis on the self as it is experienced by others. The kamikaze pilots of World War II are a good example of this value system. The snuffing out of their self-experience was considered nothing compared to the glory given their memories by their families and compatriots. Shneidman and Farberow called these "cultural" suicides.

Shneidman and Farberow looked for evidence to support their hypothesis about catalogic in suicide notes. They believed that catalogic would be evident in the notes where there is (1) concern with minor details, trivia and neutral statements; (2) concern with the indirect and direct reactions of others; (3) lack of concern with personal suffering and pain; and (4) lack of indication of belief in an afterlife. They interpreted the high frequency of detailed instructions in suicide notes as the result of the suicide's unrealistic feelings of omnipotence and omnipresence. Suicidal people cannot imagine their death and cessation and therefore think simultaneously of being absent and giving orders as though they were going to be present to enforce them. Thus, Schneidman and Farberow concluded, they are thinking unrealistically.

In another sense, it may not be so illogical to give orders when one will not be present to enforce them. If suicidal people were not aware that they would not be present after death, they would not need to give orders at all; they would assume that they could be there to arrange the details personally.

SUMMARY

Suicidologists have wondered whether suicidal individuals "think" themselves into suicidal states and suicidal actions because their distorted thought processes tell them that it's the appropriate choice of behaviors. Some research has been done on disordered deductive reasoning (called paralogic), but it seems unlikely that most nonpsychotic suicides are caused by this kind of error in thinking. It seems more probable that disordered thinking in the suicidal person is a matter of distortion of ideas rather than logic. To other people, their ideas seem rigid and conceptualized in a dichotomous fashion: everything is black or white, with no shades of gray. Suicidal persons may also make distortions of specific concepts, most notably in the way they perceive themselves.

REFERENCES

McLeavey, B.C., Daly, R.J., Ludgate, J.W. and Murray, C.M. Interpersonal problem-solving skills training in the treatment of self-poisoning patients. *Suicide and Life-Threatening Behavior* 24:382-394, 1994.

Neuringer, C. Dichotomous evaluations in suicidal individuals. *Journal of Consulting Psychology* 25:445-449, 1961.

Neuringer, C. Rigid thinking in suicidal individuals. *Journal of Consulting Psychology* 28:54-58, 1964.

Neuringer, C. The cognitive organization of meaning in suicidal individuals. *Journal of General Psychology* 76:91-100, 1967.

Schmidtke, A. and Schaller, S. The role of cognitive factors in suicidal behavior. In U. Bille-Brahe and H. Schiodt (eds.), *Intervention and Prevention*. Odense, Denmark: University of Odense, 1994.

Schotte, D. and Clum, G. Problem-solving skills in suicidal psychiatric patients. *Journal of Consulting and Clinical Psychology* 55:49-54, 1987.

Shneidman, E.S. *Suicide as Psychache*. Northvale, NJ: Jason Aronson, 1993.

Shneidman, E.S. and Farberow, N.L. *Clues to Suicide*. New York: McGraw-Hill, 1957.

Von Domarus, E. The specific laws of logic in schizophrenia. In J.S. Kasanin (ed.), *Language and Thought in Schizophrenia*. New York: W.W. Norton, 1944.

12

Gender Differences in Suicidal Behavior

Of all that is known about the phenomenon of suicide, few things are as clear as the fact that men and women differ in their suicidal behavior. Many American studies have shown that the rate of completed suicide is higher for men than for women, while women show a higher incidence of attempted suicide than do men. Shneidman and Farberow (1961), studying suicidal behavior in Los Angeles for the year 1957, found that of 768 completed suicides, 540 were male and 228 were female. Of 2,652 attempted suicides, 1,824 were female and 828 were male. These differences seem to hold for suicidal behavior in other countries as well, including Hong Kong (Yap, 1958), the Netherlands (De Graaf and Kruyt, 1976) and Israel (Shichor and Bergman, 1979).

Men and women also seem to differ in the seriousness of their suicidal behavior. Not all methods of attempting suicide carry the same probability of death. It is possible to rate suicidal acts according to their potential lethality. For example, a gunshot wound to the head is very likely to cause death, while taking an overdose of aspirin is much less likely to be fatal (it is difficult to swallow enough aspirin without inducing vomiting). Wrist-cutting is also unlikely to be lethal because pain usually prevents the individual from making a deep enough cut. Men tend to use the more lethal and women the less lethal methods.

There are also differences in the level of danger of each of the possible methods of committing suicide. People can shoot themselves through the heart, or just through a couple of ribs; they can take a large handful of tranquilizers or only a few. When men and women are compared in terms of the severity of their suicidal acts, most evidence suggests that men make the more severe attempts. The actual difference may be even more extreme than research has suggested because very mild suicidal attempts (which are most like-ly to be made by women) may never come to the attention of the authorities.

The evidence for gender differences in suicide is thus rather clearcut. We will now consider some of the explanations that have been offered for these differences.

DIFFERENCES IN MANIPULATIVE INTENT

Stengel (1964) has suggested that women attempt suicide more often than men because they use suicidal behavior as a means of manipulating relationships. Other means of exerting pressure on others, like sheer physical power or financial threats, are not as available to women as they are to men. In other words, some suicide attempts may not be flirtations with death, but rather ways of bring-ing about change in the environment. Among other things, suicidal behavior may be an effective way of expressing aggression. The lat-ter idea seems reasonable, but there is as yet little empirical evi-dence to enable us to evaluate its validity.

DIFFERENCES IN CHOICE OF METHOD

One explanation for gender differences in suicide is that women are less successful at killing themselves because they choose less lethal methods. Indeed, the Los Angeles study by Shneidman and Farberow made clear that women chose different methods for com-mitting suicide than men did. Only 14 percent of the women who completed suicide shot themselves in the head, while 35 percent of the men chose this method. Women tended to prefer taking barbi-turates and poisons and shooting themselves somewhere in the torso (in other words, not in the head). As was pointed out earlier, these methods are less likely to be fatal than others.

There are more differences than just the choice of method. Even when the method is held constant, men are more likely to succeed in killing themselves than are women. Among the suicides investi-gated by Shneidman and Farberow, 16 of 24 men who jumped from high places succeeded in killing themselves. Of 27 women using the same method, only nine died.

It has been posited that the difference in choice of method and in the success in using a particular method is due to differences in the values held by men and women. Research into gender differences in attitudes toward death (Diggory and Rothman, 1961) has suggested that women are more concerned than men with what happens to their bodies after death. Perhaps a woman's greater concern with bodily appearance is extended to appearance after death. Suicidal women might try to choose a method of suicide that would be least disfiguring. Clearly, barbiturates would be less disfiguring than a gunshot to the head or the effects of a fall from the tenth story of a building. However, the less disfiguring methods for suicide are almost always less lethal.

PHYSIOLOGICAL DIFFERENCES

One relevant difference between men and women may be the fact that there is usually a difference in physical strength. Women, being on average smaller and less muscular than men, may find it more difficult to handle the mechanical manipulations required by the more lethal suicide methods. Firing a gun accurately or plunging a knife may be more difficult for a woman than for a man, and thus less likely to be performed in a manner that causes death. Lack of physical strength may also lead women to choose suicide methods that require little exertion, like barbiturates and poisons.

A more basic difference lies in the type and level of sex hormones (estrogen, testosterone, progesterone) present in the body. Most research on this topic has focused on the relationship between hormone levels and suicide in women rather than in men. The sex hormone level in men is fairly constant over a period of several years. Women, on the other hand, provide excellent subjects for this kind of research because in almost all women of childbearing age there are considerable changes in hormone levels over short periods of time. These changes are fairly accurately reflected by the simple index of the menstrual cycle. Between the beginning of menstruation and the time of ovulation, halfway through the cycle, there is a low progesterone level and a gradually increasing level of estrogen. Following ovulation, estrogen production is decreased and the progesterone level rises abruptly, to be maintained at a high level until the next menstruation begins.

There is some evidence that the suicide rate in women differs with the stage of the menstrual cycle. After reviewing the many studies on attempted suicide and the menstrual cycle, Lester (1990) concluded that the least common time for nonfatal suicidal acts by women is in the third week of the cycle, between days 15 and 21. Not enough data had been collected from women who had completed suicide for reliable conclusions to be drawn about this group.

In pregnant women who have a high progesterone level, the suicide rate is quite low — only about one-sixth of the expected rate

(Whitlock and Edwards, 1968). Obviously, however, it can be argued that there are many factors other than hormone levels that could militate against the suicide of a pregnant woman. Becoming pregnant might in some way serve purposes similar to those of attempting suicide. For example, pregnancy may attract other people's attention and solicitude. It also leads to a new social role that may, in some cases, be more satisfying for the woman than her old role.

One final issue relevant to suicidal behavior and hormone levels is whether oral contraceptives, which change the levels of hormones, have any impact on women's suicidal behavior. The available evidence indicates that nonfatal suicide attempts may be more common among women who take oral contraceptives than among those who use diaphragms (Vessey, McPherson, Lawless and Yeates, 1985).

In animals, a close association has been observed between sex hormone levels and acts of aggression. High levels of male hormone (testosterone) are generally associated with a high level of aggressiveness. The same statement cannot be made about the female hormones, though those that bring about lactation may be associated with aggressiveness in guarding the young from intruders. Recently, Lester (1993) has noted that there is some evidence that men who have completed suicide had elevated testosterone levels. Looking at national suicide rates, Lester found that the gender difference in rates of completed suicide is found only in cases employing violent methods. For nonviolent methods such as medications and poisons, there was very little difference between the completed suicide rates of men and women. Therefore, Lester argued, testosterone may be responsible for the great volume of violent suicidal acts by men and their resulting higher suicide rate.

PSYCHOLOGICAL DIFFERENCES

Some bizarre psychological explanations have been offered for the difference in suicidal behavior between men and women. Davis (1968) suggested that the difference was due to differing strengths of religious faith in men and women. However, it is difficult to see why the religious faith of women, which presumably should keep them from completing suicide, should also not prevent them from attempting suicide so frequently.

Canetto (1992) has argued that the well-established and well-known gender norms for suicidal behavior (men committing more fatal acts and women more nonfatal acts) influence a person's choice of suicidal behavior. When the general public is surveyed, fatal (completed) suicide is repeatedly associated with the male gender and with masculinity, while nonfatal (attempted) suicide is associated with the female gender and femininity. For example, when asked to predict how they thought people would generally respond to severe crises, respondents predicted completed suicide more often for men than for women and more often for "masculine" individuals than for "feminine" individuals (Linehan, 1973).

Furthermore, among the elderly, Canetto attributed the higher completed suicide rate among men to gender differences in coping. Older women may have more flexible and diverse ways of coping than older men. Adopting different coping strategies to fit the situation is a skill that is the product of socialization and developmental experience.

Berkowitz (1961) has provided a more general hypothesis about sex difference in suicidal behavior that he bases on aggression. Suicide, of course, can be seen as an act of self-directed aggression. As was mentioned above, in most species of animals, males are more aggressive than females (and the level of male aggressiveness seems closely related to the level of testosterone). In humans, too, research seems to indicate that males are the more aggressive sex, whether aggression is measured by psychological tests or overt behavior.

Most cultural norms insist that women inhibit their aggressiveness more than men. A woman may express hostility by verbal attack, but she generally does not fight physically with an opponent. Her channels for expressing anger are more subtle than those that men are allowed to use. A woman is shamed and disapproved of if she is too sharp in her verbal attack or if she comes to physical blows with another person. Because women form their attitudes partly through modeling themselves on other women in the same culture, their aggressive behavior may be inhibited even before the motivation enters consciousness. Fear of shame may be a powerful inhibitor, but introjection of cultural norms may be even stronger.

Berkowitz has suggested that only aggression that is directed outward is inhibited. Turning aggression toward the self is one way of inhibiting its outward expression. Because women also tend to have stronger affiliative needs than men, they could satisfy two kinds of needs through attempting suicide. First, they could express the aggressiveness that cultural norms force them to inhibit, and second, they could use the act to bring themselves into more intimate contact with other people. Completing suicide would be of use only for the first motivation.

SUMMARY

It seems clear that men complete suicide much more frequently than women do, while women make the majority of nonfatal suicide attempts. These differences appear to be related to differences in choice of method used to commit suicide. Interestingly, even when women use the same method as men, they still do not succeed as often as the men do. The evidence suggests that both physiological and psychological factors are involved here, and that hormonal differences and culturally determined beliefs about aggressiveness and gender roles may be especially important.

REFERENCES

Berkowitz, L. *Aggression.* New York: McGraw-Hill, 1961.

Canetto, S.S. Gender and suicide in the elderly. *Suicide and Life-Threatening Behavior* 22:80-97, 1992.

Davis, F.B. Sex differences in suicide and attempted suicide. *Diseases of the Nervous System* 29:193-194, 1968.

De Graaf, A.C. and Kruyt, C.S. Some results of the response to a national survey of suicide and attempted suicide in the Netherlands. In *Suicide and Attempted Suicide in Young People.* Copenhagen: World Health Organization, 1976.

Diggory, J.C. and Rothman, D.Z. Values destroyed by death. *Journal of Abnormal and Social Psychology* 63:205-210, 1961.

Lester, D. Suicidal behavior in men and women. *Mental Hygiene* 53:340-345, 1969.

Lester, D. Suicide and the menstrual cycle. *Medical Hypotheses* 31:197-199, 1990.

Lester, D. Testosterone and suicide. *Personality and Individual Differences* 15:347-348, 1993.

Linehan, M.M. Suicide and attempted suicide. *Perceptual and Motor Skills* 37:31-34, 1973.

Rubenstein, R., Moses, R. and Lidz, T. On attempted suicide. *Archives of Neurology and Psychiatry* 79:103-112, 1958.

Shichor, D. and Bergman, S. Patterns of suicide among the elderly in Israel. *Gerontology* 19:487-495, 1979.

Shneidman, E.S. and Farberow, N.L. Statistical comparisons between committed and attempted suicides. In N.L. Farberow and E.S. Shneidman (eds.), *The Cry for Help.* New York: McGraw-Hill, 1961.

Stengel, E. *Suicide and Attempted Suicide.* Middlesex, England: Penguin, 1964.

Vessey, M.P., McPherson, K., Lawless, M. and Yeates, D. Oral contraception and serious psychiatric illness. *British Journal of Psychiatry* 146:45-49, 1985.

Whitlock, F.A. and Edwards, J.E. Pregnancy and attempted suicide. *Comprehensive Psychiatry* 9:1-12, 1968.

Yap, P.M. *Suicide in Hong Kong*. Hong Kong: University of Hong Kong Press, 1958.

13

Young People,
African Americans
and Native Americans

When a particular group of people demonstrates a sudden increase in suicidal behavior or continues to show a steady increase in rates of suicide, it is always important to research the trend and to determine why it is occurring and what can be done to help stop it. Three such groups will be considered in this chapter: young people, African Americans and Native Americans. The suicide rates of each of these groups have increased dramatically in recent years.

SUICIDE AMONG YOUNG PEOPLE

In the past, young people generally had a low death rate from all causes. Years ago this was largely true for suicide as well, but this is no longer the case; in the last few decades, the rate of youth suicide has increased dramatically and now it has approached epidemic proportions. In 1950, the rate for people aged 15 to 24 was 4.5 per 100,000; in the 1970s, the rates for this age group rose in 22 nations and declined in only five nations (Lester, 1988); by 1990, the rate had tripled to 13.2 per 100,000; and in 1993 it had risen to 13.5. Whereas the elderly once had the highest suicide rates of all age groups in most parts of the world, in some nations (such as Canada), young people now have the highest suicide rates (Leenaars and Lester, 1990). In the United States, suicide is the third leading cause of death for people aged 15 to 19 (following homicide and accidental deaths).

Also alarming is the fact that suicide is now being reported in very young children. In 1968, 118 American children between the ages of 5 to 14 committed suicide, a very low rate of 0.3 per 100,000 people. Gradual increases in the referrals of suicidal children to mental health services alerted the profession that a serious problem was emerging. By 1989, the childhood suicide rate had more than doubled, and in 1997, suicide advanced to the sixth leading cause of death for children in this age range. It would seem noteworthy that this trend paralleled the increased availability and use of firearms as a means of suicide; more than half of these children used firearms to kill themselves. In fact, suicide is the sixth leading cause of death for 5 to 14 year olds. Leenaars (1995) described the case of an attempted suicide by a 4-year-old boy whose parents were in the midst of a divorce. Six to 13 percent of adolescents say they have attempted suicide at least one time and 80 percent of those who complete suicide have tried before. Up to 40 percent of all adolescent attempters will try again.

Most studies have found that the rate for completed suicide in males is about 4 to 5 times what it is in females, but that females attempt suicide at least three times as often as males. Young women tend to use less lethal methods (pills and gas) and young men tend to use more lethal methods (guns and ropes). Many of the symptoms of suicidal feelings are similar to those of depression. Adults should be aware of the following signs of adolescents who may be suicidal:

- Depression and hopelessness

- Withdrawal from friends and family

- Talk of committing suicide

- Scratching and marking of the body or other acts of bodily self-destruction

- Change in eating and sleeping habits

- Loss of interest in favorite activities

- Violent or disruptive actions and rebellious behavior

- Running away from home

- Increased use of drugs and alcohol

- Unusual neglect of personal appearance

- Marked personality changes

- Persistent boredom, difficulty concentrating

- Sudden decline or improvement in schoolwork

- Frequent complaints about physical symptoms, often related to emotions, such as stomachaches, headaches and fatigue

- Loss of interest in pleasurable activities

- Not tolerating praise and rewards

- Giving away cherished personal belongings

- New involvement with high-risk activities and taking unnecessary risks

- Preoccupation with death and dying in conversation, written expressions, artwork and choice of reading material

- Collection and discussion of information on suicide methods

- Making "final" arrangements and making out a will

- Comments about not being missed if gone

Aside from concern over the reasons for the growing problem of adolescent suicide, the issue also attracts research interest because of the ways in which it differs from suicide in the rest of the population. Many of the phenomena associated with suicidal adults are not found in teenagers. For example, whereas adult suicide rates peak on Mondays and in the spring, adolescent suicide rates do not; while adult suicide rates are very low in those who are married, suicide rates are high among married adolescents (second only to those who are divorced) (Seiden, 1969). The reason for this reversal in suicide rates among those who are married is obscure. Perhaps people who marry at a young age do so to escape from the unhappy homes that are frequently part of the background of suicidal individuals. On the other hand, it may be that the intimacy of marriage creates unusual stress for spouses who are very young.

What are the causes of suicidal behavior among young people? Among the general population, suicide is associated with factors such as ill health, marital conflict and job loss — factors that are less likely to affect young people than adults. The issues that seem to affect adolescents are varied. With the onset of puberty, young people are suddenly faced with a number of issues that they have never had to deal with before. They must deal with their new sexual impulses, either by suppressing them or directing them to socially approved outlets and they must also develop behavior patterns that are appropriate for their sexual identity. Earlier in life, they had to perform a part of this task when they had to learn to dress and play like a boy or like a girl. When they start becoming sexually mature, adolescents are faced with the difficult problem of learning to behave sexually like a man or a woman during a time when very little practice in sexual expression is permitted. Adolescent suicide may be based on guilt, confusion or despair that results from failure to perform these difficult tasks "properly."

Suicidal behavior in adolescents is more often related to acute interpersonal problems, whereas suicidal behavior in older adults is more often related to long-term, chronic personal problems such as depression and medical illnesses. Suicidal behavior in adolescents seems more impulsive and, as a result, there seem to be fewer indications that the adolescent is at risk for suicide. This difficulty in anticipating suicidal behavior in adolescents is further increased by the fact that depressed adolescents do not show the same symptoms as depressed adults. Whereas depressed adults will seem apathetic, lethargic, sad and guilt-ridden, depressed adolescents may appear to be angry and show antisocial behavior.

Suicidal behavior in adolescents often seems to be influenced by family situations. Conflicts with parents, who themselves may be suicidal and psychiatrically disturbed and who create chaotic, unstable homes, are common in the family backgrounds of suicidal adolescents (Jacobs, 1971). Parental hostility toward the adolescent — even to the point of harboring unconscious wishes that their child did not exist — may play a role in the adolescent's suicidal impulses (Richman, 1986).

Modeling may play a stronger role in adolescent suicidal behavior than it does in adult suicide. Suicidal behavior in peers is much more likely to trigger imitative suicidal behavior in adolescents (Coleman, 1987), and suicidal behavior in family members, especially parents and siblings, also increases the risk of suicide in adolescents. An example of this imitative pattern can be seen in the behavior of Jody White who was the subject of a widely acclaimed book written by his mother (White-Bowden, 1985). At the age of 17, three years after his father had shot himself, Jody followed suit and committed suicide. When Jody was 14, his mother and father finally got divorced after four years of separations and reconciliations. However, Jody's father did not accept the finality of the divorce and, after trying unsuccessfully to persuade his ex-wife to reconcile one more time, he shot himself in the bedroom of his ex-wife's home. Jody's mother admitted that she did not realize the extent of the psychological distress that this may have caused her children, and she never considered getting counseling for her family. Three years later, after Jody's girlfriend broke up with him and refused to consider reconciliation, Jody went home and dealt with the situation in the exact same way as his father had; he shot and killed himself.

Suicide among college students is a special case with its own problems concerning the motivations for self-destruction. Although the suicide rate for all college students in the United States is average (Schwartz and Reifler, 1980), a number of studies have indicated that the suicide rate is higher for students who attend prestigious universities than it is for students who go to lesser colleges and for nonstudents. For example, suicide rates at Cambridge and Oxford Universities are much higher than at less prestigious British universities (21 and 26 suicides per 100,000 per year, respectively, in the 1950s, compared to 6 suicides per 100,000 at the less prestigious universities) (Lyman, 1961). The same ratio of rates is found in Japan (Ishii, 1985) and in the United States, though it is less well documented. (Ithaca, New York, the town in which Cornell University is located, has four bridges that are notorious as places from which students and others have jumped to their deaths.)

One relevant factor in college student suicide is the students' feelings of success or failure in school. Students who commit suicide tend to have relatively high grades compared to the average students (Seiden, 1966). However, their families report that most of these suicidal students never felt competent or secure about their academic success. Their families say that their children believed that their high grades were an accident and an erroneous indication of their real ability and that they felt like "frauds." This may account for the higher suicide rates at the more prestigious universities where students, who were once among the best students in their high schools, had to face fiercer competition from a whole class of equally able students. This stress, combined with the typical suicidal stressors of depression, family conflict and interpersonal problems, may make suicide more likely.

Special efforts have been made to prevent suicide among adolescents. In many communities there are telephone hotlines for distressed suicidal adolescents. These hotlines are often staffed by young people because they are sometimes more able than adults to relate to and feel empathy with distressed peers. In addition, many schools have added suicide and suicide prevention components to their health education programs (Stevenson and Stevenson, 1996). It is hoped that adolescent suicide will be prevented, or at least lessened, by informing students about the causes of suicide, the ways in which peers can respond to depressed fellow students, and the resources that are available in the community. However, it has not yet been possible to show that these programs have had a discernible effect on the rates of adolescent suicide.

SUICIDE AMONG AFRICAN AMERICANS

Suicide among African Americans, especially young men, has been viewed as a serious problem for many years. An analysis of federal statistics shows that from 1980 to 1990, the suicide rates for black males aged 15 to 24 increased 63 percent (from 12.3 to 20.1 per 100,000), compared to 8 percent (from 21.4 to 23 per 100,000) for white males in the same age group. For all racial groups and both genders of this age group during this same time period, suicide rates rose less than 10 percent. Furthermore, it is especially startling that from 1980 to 1993, for males aged 10 to 14, the suicide rate increased 358 percent for blacks, but only 73 percent for whites; for males aged 15 to 19, the rate increased 157 percent for blacks and 23 percent for whites; for those aged 20 to 24, the rate for blacks increased by 30 percent and fell 1.2 percent for whites. Special concern about this issue surfaced first in the 1960s (Seiden, 1970), and it has reemerged in the 1990s as the rates kept rising. Whereas suicide rates reach their peak fairly late in life (65 years and older) for the U.S. population as a whole, as we can see from the above statistics, the rates for African Americans increase as their age drops.

The few studies that have looked into this serious problem have proposed a variety of reasons why African American males have been taking their own lives at such increasing rates and some of them are conflicting.

Hendin (1969) considered the syndrome of "black suicide" as it relates to family problems. The frequent absence of a father in the family seems especially significant. The young African American who comes from a family with no resident father may feel a combination of rage against others and despair that he will never have the love and support of a father. There are also often difficult relations between children and mothers. A mother, especially one with children born out of wedlock, often leaves her children in the care of their grandmother or aunt while she works, moves to another town, or lives with a man who does not want the children around. The children may later be taken from these relatives, once again to live with their mother for a time. This inconsistency of care may increase the child's rage and despair: rage against the rejecting mother and despair of finding a secure place in her affection. Children who are in such a position may have feelings about their parents that may remain unresolved for a long time, sometimes till late in life. For these people, suicide may be a way to resolve these family conflicts. Suicide may also result from the distress and confusion about an inability to form adult relationships that will satisfy lingering childhood needs.

Another source of stress for urban African-American males is unemployment. Unemployment rates are extremely high for young black males, much higher than for young men of other ethnic groups. In a society where work is a measure of self-worth, it is understandable that unemployment can have such adverse effects. The result is emotional as well as financial distress, both of which cause feelings of incompetence and torpor.

On the other hand, when job opportunities do become available, statistics indicate that they may raise the suicide rate among young blacks rather than lower it. After a long period of deprivation and frustration, hopes may rise too fast and too high when a job finally does come along, causing expectations that are far beyond the satisfactions that could be realistically obtained from a job. The experience of frustration at this point could cause a much more explosive reaction and their frame of mind could be much worse than if they weren't working at all.

Seiden (1970) noted that suicidal behavior among young African Americans includes an act that is relatively rare among whites — victim-precipitated homicide. This occurs when a person makes himself a victim by provoking another person to kill him. Why would suicidal African Americans who want to commit suicide choose this method? Seiden suggested they do this because the act of suicide is considered completely unacceptable in the black community.

Suicide may be also be regarded by young black men as an unmasculine act. The young urban black male is expected (and expects himself) to be able to take the cards that life deals him without complaining or breaking down. He also typically regards violence as a reasonable way to solve problems. When he is motivated by suicidal impulses, he may decide that the best way to solve his conflicting needs is to provoke violence that will not only harm others, but will also cause his own death. This form of death will also satisfy the rage he feels toward his family in particular and society in general.

Another theory about the rise in the suicide rate among black males is that it is a byproduct of integration and the rising status of African Americans. This idea is based on the notion that as blacks become more absorbed into the white culture, they lose their family, religious and cultural ties. Before integration, black families were more intact, they lived together in a more closely tied community and they shared resources. As blacks became integrated into the white community, they may have had more rights, but perhaps they also suddenly found themselves in a world that they didn't understand well and one in which they had to compete, not only against their black peers, but also against whites.

One question that is now heard asks, Did the black males who committed suicide in the last several years have little education and come from low-income backgrounds? Or, are the deaths more prevalent among those with better educations and higher income? If they came from the latter group, it is possible that as African Americans acquire greater social status, they also assume some of the problems that are suffered by the white community. Similarly, we might ask, Does this surge in suicide stem from social ills that seem to affect black Americans disproportionately — such as poverty and drug abuse? However, if race is an explanation, how can we explain the fact that suicide rates among young black women during 1980 to 1993 have not changed and, for some age groups, have even declined (Shen, 1996)?

Another possibility for the rising suicide rate is the easy availability of firearms, noting that almost all of the suicides by black men in this time period involved guns.

The meager investigation that has been conducted on the alarming phenomenon of steadily rising suicide rates for young African American males has presented us with a good deal of information that we really cannot understand very well. There are various theories, but none of them have been well developed. It is fair to say that we are not sure why suicide rates for this group have increased, but the fact that they continue to rise should prompt not only the establishment of suicide prevention programs tailored to African Americans, but also much more serious research.

SUICIDE AMONG NATIVE AMERICANS

Suicide rates among several of the Native American tribes have been at a high level for many years. For example, the suicide rate in 1985 among Alaskan natives was 100 per 100,000 for males and 24 per 100,000 for females, compared to 24 and 7 for Alaskan white males and females, respectively (Forbes and van der Hyde, 1988). In 1992, the rate among 15 to 24 year olds was 42 per 100,000 and as high as 49 per 100,000 in 1990.

May and Van Winkle (1994) have noted that Native American tribes differ greatly in their degree of social integration. In low-integration tribes, individuals are members of few social groups other than the family or band, and these social groups do not place strong mandates on conformity. Individuals have more freedom to define their own behavior. In New Mexico, Plains tribes, such as the

Apache, have low levels of integration, the Navajo have medium levels, and the Pueblo have high levels. These tribes also differ in the extent to which they have been influenced and acculturated by modern, western and mainstream cultural life. May and Van Winkle found that the Native American tribes in New Mexico with medium levels of social integration had the lowest suicide rates, and that the tribes with higher levels of acculturation had higher suicide rates. Thus, both social integration and acculturation played a role in determining the suicide rate of the tribe.

Dizmang (1967) described the situation he found when asked to give advice on the near-epidemic rates of suicide among adolescents of the Northern Cheyenne. In premodern days, suicide was rare among the Cheyenne men in the tribe. When they were a free and well-functioning group, they had their own culturally prescribed ways of dealing with self-esteem and aggression. When a man was distressed by loss of esteem, he would deal with his emotions by organizing a small war party to raid an enemy tribe. He would either regain his self-esteem through some brave act enacted during the fight, or else he would die in the attempt. The Cheyenne women were more likely than the men to kill themselves, particularly if their marriages were unhappy or childless, and they usually did so by hanging. However, even among the Cheyenne women, suicide used to be fairly rare.

A form of self-destructive behavior common among Cheyenne men was the Sun Dance, a ritual in which the dancer thrust sharpened sticks that were first tied to a pole through his pectoral muscles. Staring at the sun, he would dance backward, sometimes until the sticks tore their way out of his muscles. This ritual, according to Dizmang, was "as important in handling aggressive feelings as going into battle with an enemy."

When the Cheyenne were placed on the reservation, these methods of handling aggression were forbidden. Because the wholesale slaughter of buffalo by whites has rendered them nearly extinct, buffalo hunting, which was another way of expressing aggression, became almost impossible. At the same time the Cheyenne's time-honored means of dealing with aggression were removed, regulations that decreased self-esteem were introduced. For example, the men were required to cut their long hair, which was a highly valued symbol of strength. Furthermore, the loss of their old way of life made it impossible for the tribe to support itself on the reservation, and the welfare programs that were introduced as a result served to further undercut self-esteem.

Dizmang attributed the high suicide rate among the Cheyenne to a loss of the traditional ways of handling aggression and loss of face, as well as to the lack of self-esteem inherent in life on the reservation. On the reservation, individuals become boxed in between their own basic needs and the impossibility of gratification in the regimented environment. Often the reaction to these situations is the abusive consumption of alcohol, severe depression, or involvement with homicide, suicide, or violent accidents.

One solution for the Cheyenne might be leaving the reservation and starting a new life on the outside. However, one of the highest Cheyenne values is loyalty to the tribe and this would be violated by leaving. In addition, there are no small Cheyenne communities off the reservation to help the "emigrant" in his transition. Between feelings of guilt about leaving the reservation and the fact that he must make a precipitous change, joining the mainstream culture becomes less and less of a viable alternative for the Cheyenne. A better alternative might be a reform of the reservation culture by improving community organization, tapping internal resources and developing a process of self-renewal.

SUMMARY

Some subgroups have particularly serious suicide problems that differ from those found in the general population. Young Americans, for whom suicide is a leading cause of death, now have suicide rates equal to or greater than those of the elderly, the group that used to be at greatest risk for suicide. Not only do adolescent suicides seem to act more impulsively than adults, but they often become suicidal in response to interpersonal crises and threats to their self-esteem from perceived academic performance. Suicide among young African Americans, especially males, seems to be a consequence of limited opportunities, racism, poverty, a high probability of chronic unemployment, and, for some groups, it is perhaps connected to issues of integration and rising status. Victim-precipitated homicide is common in this group. Native Americans on reservations have shown suicide rates of near-epidemic proportions, a problem that has been attributed to a breakdown in the traditional ways of dealing with aggression and loss of self-esteem.

REFERENCES

Barraclough, B.M. Sex ratio of juvenile suicide. *Journal of the American Academy of Child and Adolescent Psychiatry* 26:434-435, 1987.
Coleman, L. *Suicide Clusters*. Boston: Faber & Faber, 1987.
Dizmang, L. Suicide among the Cheyenne Indians. *Bulletin of*

Suicidology, July 1967, pp. 8-11.

Early, K.E. and Akers, R.L. It's a white thing. *Deviant Behavior* 14:277-296, 1993.

Forbes, N. and van der Hyde, V. Suicide in Alaska from 1978 to 1985. *American Indian and Alaska Native Mental Health Research* 1(3):36-55, 1988.

Hendin, H. *Black Suicide*. New York: Basic Books, 1969.

Ishii, K. Backgrounds of higher suicide rates among name university students. *Suicide and Life-Threatening Behavior* 15:56-68, 1985.

Jacobs, J. *Adolescent Suicide*. New York: Wiley, 1971.

Leenaars, A.A. Justin: A suicide attempt in a four-year-old boy. In A.A. Leenaars and D. Lester (eds.), *Suicide and the Unconscious*. Northvale, NJ: Jason Aronson, 1996.

Leenaars, A.A. and Lester, D. Suicide in adolescents. *Psychological Reports* 67:867-873, 1990.

Lester, D. Youth suicide. *Adolescence* 23:955-958, 1988.

Lester, D. Differences in the epidemiology of suicide in Asian Americans by nation of origin. *Omega* 29: 89-93, 1994.

Lyman, J.L. Student suicide at Oxford University. *Student Medicine* 10:260-264, 1961.

May, P.A. and Van Winkle, N.W. Durkheim's suicide theory and its applicability to contemporary American Indians and Alaska Natives. In D. Lester (ed.), *Emile Durkheim: Le Suicide 100 Years Later*. Philadelphia: The Charles Press, 1994.

Richman, J. *Family Therapy for Suicidal People*. New York: Springer, 1986.

Schwartz, A.J. and Reifler, C.B. Suicide among American college and university students from 1970-1971 through 1975-1976. *Journal of the American College Health Association* 28:205-210, 1980.

Seiden, R.H. Campus tragedy. *Journal of Abnormal Psychology* 71:389-399, 1966.

Seiden, R.H. *Suicide among Youth*. Washington, DC: U.S. Public Health Service, 1969.

Seiden, R.H. We're driving young blacks to suicide. *Psychology Today* 4(3):24-28, 1970.

Shen, F. Where suicide rates are soaring. *The Washington Post* July 29-August 4, 1996.

Stevenson, R.G. and Stevenson, E.P. (eds.). *Teaching Students about Death*. Philadelphia: The Charles Press, 1996.

White-Bowden, S. *Everything to Live For*. New York: Poseidon, 1985.

14

Sociological Factors in Suicide

Throughout this book we have spent a lot of time considering intrapersonal and interpersonal correlates of suicide. It is also important to look at some of the external circumstances that can cause people to want to commit suicide. We have looked at the effects of gender difference, which like other nonpsychological factors, is not itself a cause of suicide, but when combined with other factors, it may contribute to a psychological state that can lead to suicide. In this chapter we will examine a number of other external circumstances, which — like gender — do not directly cause suicide, but which may contribute to the development of suicidal tendencies. In the case of each of these variables, the interaction that leads to suicide is very complex. We cannot use demographic factors to make predictions about the suicidal tendencies of any one person, but when we look at large groups of people, we may find differences in suicide rates that seem dependent upon some external factor, such as social class.

In discussing demographic variables, I will make use of three different categories: (1) static variables — circumstances that do not change over a given period of time, such as place of residence; (2) dynamic environmental variables — changes that are taking place in the world, such as war; and (3) dynamic personal variables — changes in the individual relative to the world, such as alterations in social status.

STATIC VARIABLES

Place of Residence

The question of whether suicide rates are higher in urban or rural areas has produced conflicting research results. Alexander's team (1982) found no urban-rural differences in South Carolina, but

Pasewark and Fleer (1981) found higher rates in urban Wyoming. Jarosz (1978) found no urban-rural differences in Poland and other Eastern European nations, while Fusé (1980) found higher suicide rates in rural Japan. The methods used for suicide also differ, with firearms more popular as a method for suicide in rural areas than in urban areas (Baker et al., 1984).

When the rural suicide rate is low, its level is usually attributed to the greater stability of the rural family, the larger number of children and the unified interests and traditions of rural families (Lester, 1992). Increases in rural suicide rates are attributed to the increasing social isolation of country life, as well as the disruption of traditional rural life by urban values.

Research by Shneidman and Farberow (1960) examined differences in suicidal behavior in the various residential areas of Los Angeles County. They divided the county into 100 subareas, which they classified into three socioeconomic statuses and three types of communities. They then examined the suicide notes written in each type of community and found a number of differences.

In the most economically advantaged suburbs, the suicide notes that were examined stressed reasons for the suicide rather than simply expressing emotions. The most common reasons were weariness, boredom and dissatisfaction with life. People from the most advantaged apartment-house areas stressed ill health as the reason for suicide; the emotional tone was one of guilt, and they asked for forgiveness for their act. Schneidman and Farberow gave the following example of the unemotional sort of note left in the advantaged suburbs (p. 283):

No funeral. Please leave the body to science. William Smith.

In the advantaged apartment-house areas, the notes mentioned ill health and asked for forgiveness, as in the following note (p. 284):

To all my friends: Please forgive me and thanks for all your kindness. My courage has run out. In the face of poor health, deserted by my sisters, and persistent cruelty of my husband, I have no further reason to keep fighting. All my life I have tried to be decent. I have worked hard to make a marriage out of puny material. To be deserted at such a time of my life is more than I can bear.

In moderately advantaged suburbs, the motivational pattern as seen in suicide notes rarely expressed guilt or fears about poor health. Conflicts between love and hate were most commonly expressed. Here is a typical note written by a person from such an area (p. 285):

> Mary: Here is the note you wanted, giving you power of attorney for the house and everything else (including all your bills). I hope that my insurance will get you out of the whole mess that you got us both in. This isn't hard for me to do because it's probably the only way I'll ever get rid of you, we both know how the California courts see only the women's side...I think that Junior and Betty and George are really the only good things in the world that I'll miss. Please take good care of them. Good Luck, Bill.

In the moderately advantaged "little cities" of Los Angeles County, suicide notes contained few expressions of affection toward the recipient. Instead there was anger and a feeling of having been rejected. The least advantaged industrial areas yielded notes that were matter-of-fact instructions about the disposal of the body and material possessions, reminiscent of the unemotional tone of the notes from the most advantaged suburbs.

Age

Much of our traditional mythology about suicide has regarded self-destruction as a tragedy associated with the emotional intensity of the adolescent years. Literary representations of suicide, such as Goethe's young Werther and Shakespeare's Romeo and Juliet, have strengthened this view. In actuality, for most nations, the suicide rate increases with age. In the United States, the rate for men continues to rise throughout the life span, whereas the rate for women reaches its peak somewhere between 45 and 65 years of age. In recent years, however, because the suicide rates for the young have been rising, there is often a secondary peak for those 15 to 24 years of age.

In the United States in 1988, the highest suicide rate was for men aged 75 and older (57.8 per 100,000 per year), but there was a secondary peak for those aged 25 to 34 (25 per 100,000 per year). The suicide rate for women was highest in those aged 45 to 54 (7 to 9 per 100,000 per year). In contrast, in Hungary the suicide rates for both men and women rose consistently with age (Lester, 1994c).

When we compare the suicidal behavior of older people with that of younger adults, we find many differences. The younger people are more likely to attempt suicide than the older group. Even when older people attempt suicide, their methods are more lethal (i.e., more likely to cause death) than those of the younger attempters, and so their attempts are more serious.

The motives of older suicidal people have been investigated by looking at their suicide notes (Farberow, and Shneidman, 1957; Leenaars, 1994). As the age of the suicidal individuals increases, there is less motivation for self-punishment or revenge, and more evidence of a wish to escape discomfort and pain. The suicides of younger adults are more often impulsive and more often precipitated by a specific interpersonal problem. This is less likely with older suicidal individuals for whom the most frequent disturbing event is a serious medical illness or a problem with surgery or medical treatment. Other stressful factors for the elderly may include the death of friends, changes of residence, and job or financial problems (Lester, 1994a).

Societal Attitude Toward Suicide

Societies differ markedly in their approval or disapproval of suicidal behavior. Several suicidologists (e.g., Farber, 1968) have suggested that the attitude of a given society or dominant group may make a difference in the suicide rate. Differences in learned attitude may account, in part, for the low suicide rate among Roman Catholics as compared to Protestants, and for the variations that exist in the suicide rate among the Scandinavian countries (see Chapter 4), where Norway has a lower suicide rate than Sweden and Denmark.

Unemployment

There is strong evidence that suicide rates are higher among the unemployed. This association has been found in studies of the unemployment rate of societies as a whole and in individual case studies, as well as in studies over regions and over time, and for both completed and attempted suicide (Platt, 1984, 1986).

The reasons for this association may be complex. Unemployment is often an additional stressor for people, and when combined with other stressors and particular personal inclinations, it can increase the risk of suicide. Then too, dysfunctional people may be more likely to be fired from their jobs (and less likely to be rehired) and also are more likely to attempt or complete suicide. People with a psychiatric disorder are less likely to have a stable work record and more likely to become suicidal. Platt and Duffy (1986) found that unemployed men who attempted suicide more often were unmarried, manual workers (rather than skilled workers), more often were drug abusers and more often had a criminal record than employed suicide attempters.

Occupational Status and Occupation

Even though an old study (Labovitz and Hagedorn, 1971) found no association between the suicide rate and the "prestige" of an occupation, newer data suggest that people in certain occupations do indeed commit suicide more often than those in others. Blue-collar jobs, for example, are associated with higher suicide rates. In Sacramento, California from 1925 to 1979, suicide rates were higher for farm laborers, general laborers and service workers (Lampert et al., 1984). In Detroit too, suicide rates were higher for laborers and factory workers (Stack, 1980).

It appears that even if status is kept constant, people in certain occupations commit suicide more frequently than others. It has been suggested (Farber, 1968) that those whose profession involves giving nurturance and help to others have an increased suicide rate. For example, of all types of physicians, the group with the highest suicide rate is psychiatrists, who in some ways are faced with the greatest demand for interpersonal giving. The suicide rates of service workers (such as policemen and nurses) also seem to be higher than those of craftsmen (such as carpenters and tailors).

DYNAMIC ENVIRONMENTAL VARIABLES

The Economy

Jokes, cartoons and anecdotes have fostered the idea that there were many suicides (especially among upper-class males) following the stock market crash of October 1929. In fact, the suicide rate for the month following the crash was the same as that a year earlier and a year later (Galbraith, 1954).

There are three theories about the possible relationship of suicide rates and the state of the economy: that the suicide rate increases as the economy improves, that the suicide rate increases as the economy worsens, and that the suicide rate increases as the economy either improves or worsens. The evidence seems to support this last possibility, though the results depend on which measure of the economy (such as unemployment and growth in the gross national product) is used (Lester and Yang, 1995). It appears that the economy acts as a dynamic variable rather than as a static variable, and that changes in the economy affect suicidal behavior. In general, suicide rates increase as the economy worsens.

The Effects of War

We all know that war has many different effects on people. It may free some individuals to act out aggressive fantasies and allow others a moratorium on career decisions. For some people, war may be such a shattering event that they spend the rest of their lives trying to resolve the feelings it engendered. For some women whose husbands go away to war, it may be a chance to break away from social constraints by getting out of the home, and for others it may be a time of unending anxiety. With all these psychodynamic functions of war, one can safely predict that suicide rates would change during the years of conflict.

The international suicide rate decreased during both the First and the Second World Wars. It decreased for both men and women, and in both participating and nonparticipating nations (Lester, 1994b).

A number of theories have been proposed to explain the decrease in suicide rates during major wars (Rojcewicz, 1971). One hypothesis is that the decrease in the male suicide rate is deceptive because suicide-prone soldiers can act out their self-destructive impulses by deliberately getting themselves killed in battle; their deaths are not recorded as suicides. However, this hypothesis only concerns combatants; it does not explain the drop in female suicide rates, nor does it explain the drop in suicide rates for those nations not participating in the war.

A second hypothesis derives from the idea that suicide is aggression turned against the self (for a detailed discussion of this idea, see Chapter 7). War makes the display of outward-directed aggression legitimate. Because the increase in outward aggression should lower the level of repressed aggressiveness, there should be a reduction in the need to attack the self. Again, this would not explain the decrease in the suicide rates of neutral nations.

The third hypothesis about the wartime suicide rate is the one suggested by the French sociologist, Emile Durkheim. Durkheim (1897) proposed that because the social integration of a society increases during war, the likelihood of suicide is lessened. This idea is supported by the decrease in suicide rates in both men and women and in both nations at war and those remaining neutral. It also explains the decrease in the French suicide rate during the Occupation, when people's greatest concern was solidarity in their resistance to the Germans. Suicide rates were reportedly low in the

Nazi concentration camps, where individuality was attacked while group identification was emphasized (Kwiet, 1984). The decrease in the military suicide rate during wartime could also result from the increased social integration as groups of soldiers become unified during combat.

Community Growth

A changing community can lead to personal disturbance for many community members. People may find that the neighborhoods in which they have lived for many years now have a drastically changed character. A family may find itself socially isolated among families of different ethnic background or social class. Older people may find that the landmarks of their childhood have disappeared, leaving them in a place that seems foreign to them.

In a study of 50 Massachusetts towns, Wechsler (1961) found that the towns that were growing rapidly had high rates of depressive disorder and suicide. According to Quinney (1965), those countries where urbanization or industrialization is increasing rapidly have also experienced increased suicide rates but relatively lower homicide rates.

Social Disorganization

The term social disorganization refers to the many factors that affect a community, such as overcrowding, the infant mortality rate and the incidence of juvenile delinquency. Social disorganization may come about as a result of rapid population change, loss of employment, or the appearance of more subtle variables such as environmental deterioration or worsening disease patterns.

The precise relation of the suicide rate to criteria of social disorganization seems to depend on which area is being studied. In Edinburgh, Scotland, rates of both attempted and completed suicide were found to be high in areas that were overcrowded, had a high rate of juvenile delinquency, a high divorce rate and many reports of cruelty to children. There was no apparent association between a high suicide rate and the incidence of infant mortality, rent-collection problems, eviction notices, or police warnings for disturbing the peace (Philip and McCulloch, 1966; McCulloch and Philip, 1967).

In Buffalo, New York, a very different picture was found (Lester, 1970). No relationships were discovered between the rate of completed suicide and overcrowding or incidence of juvenile delinquency. The completed suicide rate was high where there was a high percentage of elderly people, college-educated people and widowed or divorced people.

In Santiago, Chile, still another pattern was found (Chuaqui et al. 1966). The incidence of completed suicide correlated positively with population density and negatively with infant mortality. In other words, suicide was frequent where the population was highly crowded, but infrequent where the death rate for infants was high. This is surprising because in many cities, overcrowding and high infant mortality are positively associated with completed suicide.

An earlier study of suicide in London, England, Sainsbury (1955) gave a different set of results. Overcrowding seemed to have no influence on the suicide rate. Where poverty was frequent, the suicide rate was low; where there was a large percentage of middle-class individuals, it was high. A high incidence of completed suicide was found in areas where many people lived alone, where there were many immigrants and where the divorce and illegitimacy rates were high. The incidence of juvenile delinquency was not found to be related to the suicide rate.

Obviously, the data from these studies are in conflict. Completed suicide did not correlate with infant mortality in Edinburgh, but they were negatively related in Santiago. Overcrowding correlated with the suicide rate in Edinburgh and Santiago, but not in London or Buffalo. These inconsistencies could mean that the relationships between the suicide rate and the factors we have listed are too weak to be useful for an understanding of suicide, or they could mean that suicidal behavior is determined differently in London, Edinburgh, Buffalo and Santiago. The latter alternative could well be the case, since cross-cultural studies seem to indicate that suicide has different motivations in different cultures (Headley, 1983; Sainsbury and Barraclough, 1968). However, at the moment, it is impossible to know which alternative is correct.

Looking at an institution rather than a city, Kahne (1968) found some interesting associations. In the psychiatric hospital he studied there was a relationship between population instability and the occurrence of suicide in the patients. Months in which patients committed suicide followed periods of high turnover in staff and patient populations. When personnel quit their jobs or patients were discharged, there was no effect on the incidence of patient suicides. However, the influx of new staff and patients into the hospital seemed to be the crucial factor. Bringing in new people may have created social disorganization, which in turn affected some individuals to the extent that the likelihood of their suicide was greater.

DYNAMIC PERSONAL VARIABLES

Suicide and Emigration

People who emigrate to a new country or migrate to a new city find themselves having to adapt to their new situation. Their housing situation may differ from what they are used to, and they may be faced with a whole set of new customs, new languages and new foods. Above all, they will have to make new friends, get used to a new job and create for themselves a new niche in the social structure. It may take years before they truly feel at home in their new environment. The period of adaptation may be still further extended if the emigrants left their homeland against their will and if they cling to their old ways in a desperate attempt to retain their identity.

The completed suicide rate of immigrants to the United States is greater than that of native-born citizens, and also greater than the rates in the immigrants' home countries (Sainsbury and Barraclough, 1968). Communist Hungary had one of the highest suicide rates in the world, and Hungarian immigrants to America have shown suicide rates higher than those of other immigrant groups (see Temesváry, 1994).

Immigrants may have many reasons to escape from what has become for them an intolerable environment. Perhaps it is also the case that those who emigrate are predisposed to suicide as a means for escape. They may have left their native country because of a tendency to escape from problems rather than trying to solve them. Suicide may appear to be the only means of escape left when these people find that they have run as far as they can and still have problems.

Change in Social Class

When people experience a rise or fall in social status, their environment may seem as foreign to them as if they had migrated to another country. (James Baldwin titled his book that describes the cultural differences between Harlem and fashionable Manhattan, *Another Country*.) Completed suicides have frequently experienced recent downward social mobility, although upward mobility is found as well (Breed, 1963; Porterfield and Gibbs, 1960). In the case of suicides who were upwardly mobile, we might attribute their acts to relative social isolation within their new class, though such people might also be pushed to suicide by some real or anticipated failure in their performance. Downwardly mobile people may also be socially isolated. However, it may be that their general inability to cope with the world, which culminated in their suicide, was also instrumental in bringing about their fall in social class.

SUMMARY

Whether static or dynamic, demographic factors seem to have an effect on individual lives in such a way that they affect the suicide rate. From the content of suicide notes, we can see that a place of residence can affect a person's suicidal motivation. The elderly generally have higher suicide rates than younger adults in most parts of the world, and their motivation for suicide is most often the result of psychological or physical pain, rather than interpersonal conflict. Unemployment is associated with a higher suicide rate, while war seems to decrease the risk of suicide. Communities that are either growing rapidly or socially disorganized have higher suicide rates than more stable societies. Foreign immigrants and those who have changed social status also have an increased risk of suicide.

REFERENCES

Alexander, G., Gibbs, T., Massey, R. and Altekruse, J. South Carolina's suicide mortality in the 1970s. *Public Health Reports* 97:476-482, 1982.

Baker, S.P., O'Neill, B. and Karpf, R.S. *The Injury Fact Book*. Lexington, MA: D.C. Heath, 1984.

Breed, W. Occupational mobility and suicide among white males. *American Sociological Review* 28:178-188, 1963.

Chuaqui, C., Lemkau, P.V., Legarreta, A. and Contreras, M.A. Suicide in Santiago, Chile. *Public Health Reports* 81:1109-1117, 1966.

Durkheim, E. *Le Suicide*. Paris: Felix Alcan, 1897.

Farber, M.L. *Theory of Suicide*. New York: Funk and Wagnalls, 1968.

Farberow, N.L. and Shneidman, E.S. Suicide and age. In E.S. Shneidman and N.L. Farberow (eds.), *Clues to Suicide*. New York: McGraw-Hill, 1957.

Fus≥, T. To be or not to be. *Stress* 1(3):18-25, 1980.

Galbraith, J.K. *The Great Crash of 1929*. Boston: Houghton-Mifflin, 1954.

Headley, L.A. *Suicide in Asia and the Near East*. Berkeley: University of California Press, 1983.

Jarosz, M. Suicides in Poland. *Polish Sociological Bulletin* 2(42):87-100, 1978.

Kahne, M.J. Suicide in mental hospitals. *Journal of Health and Social Behavior* 9:255-266, 1968.

Kwiet, K. The ultimate refuge. *Leo Baeck Institute Yearbook* 29:135-168, 1984.

Labovitz, S. and Hagedorn, R. An analysis of suicide rates among occupational categories. *Sociological Inquiry* 41:67-72, 1971.

Lampert, D., Bourque, L. and Kraus, J. Occupational status and suicide. *Suicide and Life-Threatening Behavior* 14:254-269, 1984.

Leenaars, A.A. Suicide across the lifespan with particular reference to the elderly. In D. Lester and M. Tallmer (eds.), *Now I Lay Me Down: Suicide in the Elderly*. Philadelphia: The Charles Press, 1994.

Lester, D. Social disorganization and suicide. *Social Psychiatry* 5:175-176, 1970.

Lester, D. *Why People Kill Themselves*, Ed. 3. Springfield, IL: Charles C Thomas, 1992.

Lester, D. Are there unique features of suicide in adults of different ages and developmental stages? *Omega* 29:337-348, 1994a.

Lester, D. Suicide rates before, during and after the world wars. *European Psychiatry* 9:262-264, 1994b.

Lester, D. Suicide in the elderly. In D. Lester and M. Tallmer (eds.), *Now I Lay Me Down: Suicide in the Elderly*. Philadelphia: The Charles Press, 1994c.

Lester, D. and Yang, B. *The Economy and Suicide*. New York: AMS Press, 1995.

McCulloch, J.W. and Philip, A.E. Social variables in attempted suicide. *Acta Psychiatrica Scandinavica* 43:341-346, 1967.

Pasewark, R.A. and Fleer, J.L. Suicide in Wyoming, 1960-1975. *Journal of Rural Community Psychology* 2(1):39-41, 1981.

Philip, A.E. and McCulloch, J.W. Use of social indices in psychiatric epidemiology. *British Journal of Preventive and Social Medicine* 20:122-126, 1966.

Platt, S.D. Unemployment and suicidal behavior. *Social Science and Medicine* 19:93-115, 1984.

Platt, S.D. Parasuicide and unemployment. *British Journal of Psychiatry* 149:401-405, 1986.

Platt, S.D. and Duffy, J.C. Social and clinical correlates of unemployment in two cohorts of male parasuicides. *Social Psychiatry* 21:17-24, 1986.

Porterfield, A.L. and Gibbs, J.P. Occupational prestige and social mobility of suicides in New Zealand. *American Journal of Sociology* 66:147-152, 1960.

Quinney, R. Suicide, homicide, and economic development. *Social Forces* 43:401-406, 1965.

Rojcewicz, S.J. War and suicide. *Life-Threatening Behavior* 1:46-54, 1971.

Sainsbury, P. *Suicide in London*. London: Chapman & Hall, 1955.

Sainsbury, P. and Barraclough, B.M. Differences between suicide rates. *Nature* 220:1252, 1968.

Shneidman, E.S. and Farberow, N.L. A socio-psychological investigation of suicide. In H.P. David and J.C. Brengelman (eds.), *Perspectives in Personality Research*. New York: Springer, 1960.

Stack, S. Occupational status and suicide. *Aggressive Behavior* 6:233-234, 1980.

Temesváry, B. Helping the suicidal elderly: a Hungarian perspective. In D. Lester and M. Tallmer (eds.), *Now I Lay Me Down: Suicide in the Elderly*. Philadelphia: The Charles Press, 1994.

Wechsler, H. Community growth, depressive disorders, and suicide. *American Journal of Sociology* 67:9-16, 1961.

15

Sociological Theories of Suicide

Sociologists have tried to develop theories to explain why the frequency of suicide is different in different populations. The examination of the differences in the suicide rates of different societal groups was originated by the French sociologist, Emile Durkheim in 1897. He attempted to justify the use of a sociological approach by showing that social factors could predict suicide rates. Because the suicide rates of societies and groups within societies have tended to remain relatively stable over time, it suggests that the rates are reliable and amenable to study.

In this chapter, we will examine some of the most important sociological theories of suicide. We will also look at some of the research that has attempted to test predictions derived from these theories.

DURKHEIM'S THEORY

Without Durkheim, there would not be a "sociology of suicide." His theory is the predecessor of all sociological approaches to suicide. Most of the other theories we will examine here are modernizations or reformulations of Durkheim's ideas. Part of the continued interest in developing Durkheim's theory stems from the fact that Durkheim was so vague when he defined the variables in his original theory that disagreements as to what Durkheim intended to say carry on and on (Gibbs, 1994).

The basic concepts in Durkheim's analysis involve four etiological types of suicidal behavior. The first pair, egoistic suicide and altruistic suicide, is based on the idea of the level of integration of a societal group. Durkheim himself did not give a very clear definition of what he meant by social integration, but, over the years, other scholars have tried to interpret his ideas (Lester, 1994). A society is integrated to the extent that its members possess shared beliefs and sentiments, an interest in one another and a common sense of devotion to shared goals. Social integration increases when members of the group have more durable and stable social relationships. Suicidal behavior is common in societies in which there is a high degree of social integration (*altruistic suicide*) and in societies in which there is a low degree of social integration (*egoistic suicide*). Societies with a moderate degree of social integration have the lowest suicide rates. Egoistic suicide results from excessive individualism which is caused by weak family and parental ties, weak political affiliations, or religions with weak group ties. When the social ties in a society are minimal, suicide becomes more likely. At the other extreme of social integration — when people can be too closely identified with a particular group — they may then take their lives as a religious sacrifice or as the result of political or military causes and allegiances.

Durkheim based the second pair of suicidal motivations on the variable of social regulation. A society is regulated to the extent that it controls the emotions and motivations of individual members. *Fatalistic suicide* is common in societies with a high degree of social regulation, while *anomic suicide* occurs most frequently in societies with a low degree of social regulation. As with social integration, societies with a moderate degree of social regulation have the lowest incidence of suicidal behavior. When the social regulation in a society is low, people's emotions become extreme and their motivations grow too quickly, especially among business people and investors during economic booms and depressions, and among the widowed and divorced; in these situations anomic suicide becomes more common. When social regulation is high, people's hopes for the future may become thwarted, leaving them hopeless, and the result can be fatalistic suicide which is found among childless married women, very young husbands and the politically repressed.

Durkheim's statements were often so unclear that it is hard for the modern reader to understand exactly what he meant. There are, for example, two ways of interpreting Durkheim's ideas on the relationship between social behavior, shared sentiments and beliefs (also called social meanings), and the occurrence of suicide. One interpretation argues that social behavior is the cause of social meanings and hence of suicide: the structure of the society shapes the patterns of social interaction, which in turn determine the degree of social integration, and this level of social integration determines the type and frequency of suicidal behavior.

This is the interpretation of Durkheim's theory that is most accepted by American sociologists. J.D. Douglas (1967), however, took a different view: he suggested that social meanings cause social behavior and hence suicide. Douglas felt that even though Durkheim vacillated between the two positions, he ultimately accepted the second (that is, Douglas'). In this second interpretation, anomie and egoism are orientations toward the social meanings that constitute society — orientations such as aloofness, submissiveness or rebelliousness — and it is the social meanings that are the primary cause of suicidal behavior.

Durkheim never concerned himself with the problem of how to detect and understand the social meanings present in a given situation. He assumed that social meanings are always immediately obvious to the sociologists who are members of the society they are studying. Durkheim felt that there was no need to provide empirical support for the conclusions reached by sociologists because they were correct. Unfortunately, social meanings are different for differing subgroups of a society (such as specific age groups or religious factions). A sociologist cannot belong to all different subgroups, so he is bound to misunderstand the social meanings that are present in some situations. In considering empirical data, Durkheim appears to have applied whichever social meanings made the data fit the theory, even when he was aware that some commonsense interpretations were completely contrary to his own.

Durkheim's approach can be criticized in many ways, although the faults can be attributed more to his era than to the man himself. He interpreted information in ways that would support his theory. His statistical analyses were naive by modern standards. He failed to give clear definitions of his concepts and to provide guidelines for operationalizing the theoretical elements. The theory ended by being so flexible that it was irrefutable (Phillips, Ruth and MacNamara, 1994). Nonetheless, Durkheim's influence on sociological studies of suicide has been profound. Almost every new contribution by a sociologist has attempted to clarify, develop or modify some part of Durkheim's theory.

Before looking at some of these modifications, let us briefly examine two issues: (1) whether Durkheim's theory ever has been tested and (2) the nature of social integration and social regulation.

Has Durkheim's Theory Ever Been Tested?

Because there have been scores of sociological studies that have examined Durkheim's theory of suicide, the question of whether Durkheim's theory has ever been tested seems, on the surface, to be absurd. But there are two requirements for Durkheim's theory to be tested. The first is that suicidal acts must be categorized into anomic, egoistic, altruistic and fatalistic types. This has never been done. Sociological tests of Durkheim's theory have focused on the official suicide rates of regions or subgroups of the population and have never concerned themselves with assigning the suicides to the four types described by Durkheim.

The second requirement concerns the two social dimensions involved in Durkheim's theory: social integration and social regulation. Each has at least three main levels: high, moderate and low. Societies can be classified according to the determined level of these two dimensions. Research to test Durkheim's theory must therefore measure these two dimensions in the sample of societies, and classify the societies using a three-by-three matrix on the basis of their social integration and social regulation scores.

Let us examine one such study. In a sample of 53 modern nations, Lester (1989) used religious freedom and political and civil rights to measure their level of social regulation, and birth and marriage rates to measure their level of social integration. Those nations with moderate levels of both social integration and social regulation should have the lowest suicide rate, while those nations with extreme (either high or low) levels of both social integration and social regulation should have the highest suicide rates.

The results provided some support for Durkheim's theory, if we can assume that the operational measures of social integration and social regulation are valid. Nations that scored high on both social dimensions and those that scored low on both dimensions did have the highest suicide rates. However, nations with high scores on one of the social dimensions and low scores on the other did not have particularly high suicide rates; in one case (low social integration and high social regulation) the suicide rate of the group of nations was lower than that of the group of nations with moderate scores on both social dimensions. Lester concluded that low levels of social regulation and high levels of social regulation seemed to be particularly conducive to high societal suicide rates.

The Nature of Social Regulation and Social Integration

Steve Taylor (1990) argued that although Durkheim examined the relationship between specific social indices (such as the divorce rate) and suicide rates, he believed that the identified associations revealed a common underlying cause of suicide — namely, social integration and social regulation. Durkheim was searching for underlying and unobservable mechanisms and causes of suicide. Later research has shown that divorce and suicide rates are positively associated. In general, societies with higher divorce rates have higher suicide rates. Some modern sociologists have concluded that divorce *causes* suicide. Taylor argued instead that social integration and social regulation, for which divorce rates are one possible social indicator, are the causative elements in suicide.

Ferenc Moksony (1990) made a similar point. He noted that sociological studies often assume that regions with a high proportion of divorced people have higher suicide rates because of the suicides committed by these divorced people. This is a *compositional* explanation; it holds that the composition of a society causes its suicide rate. Moksony noted that when the proportion of divorced people in a region is high, suicide rates tend to be high among the single and the married population as well as the divorced. Moksony concluded that the proportion of divorced people is better treated as an index of some abstract characteristic of a society.

REFORMULATIONS OF DURKHEIM'S THEORY

Johnson's Approach

Barclay Johnson (1965) tried to demonstrate that Durkheim's four suicidal types were logically reducible to a single one. Johnson believed that the categories of altruistic and fatalistic suicide were dispensable, since almost all of Durkheim's examples of these were premodern and poorly documented. Durkheim himself considered fatalistic suicide to be quite infrequent and unimportant — in fact, he relegated it to a single footnote.

More importantly, Johnson attempted to show that egoism and anomie are identical. In Durkheim's analysis, the two states generally occurred together. He even stated explicitly that anomie and egoism are "usually merely two different aspects of one social state" (Durkheim, 1951, p. 228). If the two variables coincide empirically almost all of the time, it would be redundant to consider them separately. In addition, Johnson regarded the two concepts as conceptually one and the same. He extracted from Durkheim's work three essential features of egoism: lack of interaction among the members of a society, lack of common conscience or goals, and lack of social regulation. The last, of course, is the same as anomie.

Johnson thus arrived at a simple restatement of Durkheim's complex theory in terms of a single variable. The more integrated or regulated a society or social group becomes, the lower its suicide rate will be. Of course, Johnson's efforts were directed only toward a logical reduction of Durkheim's theory to its basic elements. The neatness of the conclusion is not a substitute for empirical support. However, recent research has tended to confirm that as indices of social integration and regulation (such as divorce rates, interregional migration and religiosity) decrease, suicide rates increase (Stack, 1989), just as Johnson's version of Durkheim's theory predicts.

Powell's Approach

E.H. Powell (1958) proposed a theory of suicide based on a reformulation of Durkheim's concept of anomie. The basic idea was that the incidence of suicide varies with social status — the position held by an individual in an organized social system. People's goals are set for them by their social status. If they cannot accept these predetermined goals, a condition of anomie results. The subjective feeling of this state includes feelings of emptiness, apathy and meaninglessness.

So far, Powell's theory is much like Durkheim's. However, he departed radically from the older theory by proposing that there are two distinct forms of anomie. *Anomie of dissociation*, a characteristic of the lower classes, is a dissociation of the self from the culture's conceptual system. The reaction to confronting chaos (the world as seen without a conceptual system) is fear, which results in flight and aggression. On the other hand, *anomie of envelopment*, which is characteristic of the upper classes, involves the envelopment of the self by the culture. There is a lack of spontaneity, a result of an unexamined commitment to the prevailing conceptual framework. Either form of anomie raises an individual's probability of suicide.

Nevertheless, new names do not make a new theory. Upon comparing Powell's two forms of anomie with Durkheim's concepts, we may note that anomie of dissociation is practically the same as Durkheim's idea of anomie, while anomie of envelopment appears to be identical with Durkheim's idea of fatalism. Thus Powell's approach did not really take matters any further than Durkheim had gone.

Ginsberg's Approach

R.B. Ginsberg (1966) reinterpreted the idea of anomie in terms of a psychological rather than a sociological concept. He related anomie to "level of aspiration," the ambitiousness of a person's goals or intentions. In Durkheim's concept, anomie resulted when lack of social restraints allowed a person's desires to grow without control, and to become insatiable.

Ginsberg agreed that anomie arises from the unhappiness or dissatisfaction of individuals. He postulated that anomie was a direct function of dissatisfaction, which was in turn a function of the difference between satisfactions received and one's level of aspiration. In the normal process there are internalized social norms, dependent on people's social position, which regulate changes in their level of aspiration. The level of aspiration thus remains proportional to the rewards, and people feel relatively satisfied. In the anomic process, on the other hand, there are no constraints on the level of aspiration, and it runs ahead of the rewards, resulting in unhappiness for the individual.

Ginsberg suggested that appropriate changes in aspiration level occur only if people see the relationship between what they do and the rewards they receive. In other words, in order for aspiration level to be flexible, people must have a sense of efficacy, a feeling that they can affect the world. Their aspiration level will increase when they come to believe that through their own efforts they can gain higher rewards in the future. It will decrease when they believe rewards will fall in the future.

It is notable that Ginsberg's approach, like that of Powell and Johnson, dealt only with reformulating Durkheim's concepts. None of them have explained exactly why anomie should lead to suicide in particular, rather than simply stating that dissatisfaction and unhappiness may be direct causes of suicide.

Gibbs and Martin's Theory of Status Integration

J.P. Gibbs and W.T. Martin (1964) held that Durkheim's theory was inadequate in many ways. They agreed with previous theorists that the distinction between anomie and egoism was slight. They also criticized Durkheim for his failure to give operational definitions of social regulation and integration or to correlate any measure of social regulation and integration with suicide rates. Gibbs and Martin worked to remedy Durkheim's omission and to develop an improved sociological theory of suicide. They stated their theory in five postulates.

First, they proposed that the suicide rate of a population varies inversely with the stability and durability of the social relationships in that population. Since sociological knowledge about social relationships is not advanced enough to allow stability and durability to be tested directly, they proposed a second related idea, namely that the stability and durability of social relationships vary directly with the extent to which people conform to the patterned and socially sanctioned demands and expectations placed upon them by others.

The demands and expectations of others make up a person's social role. People with a particular status have to conform to a certain role if they want to maintain stable social relationships. But because almost all people maintain several statuses simultaneously, they may come into conflict about how they should act. It is hard, for example, to act like both a father and a son at the same time. When conformity to one role interferes with conformity to another, people have difficulty maintaining their social relationships. This leads to Gibbs and Martin's third postulate — that the extent to which people conform to the demands and expectations placed upon them by others varies inversely with the extent to which they are confronted with role conflicts.

If two statuses with conflicting roles are occupied simultaneously, they are incompatible. This idea is summed up in the fourth postulate — that the extent to which people are confronted with role conflict varies directly with the extent to which they occupy incompatible statuses.

Finally, Gibbs and Martin proposed that the extent to which people occupy incompatible statuses varies inversely with their degree of status integration. By means of the five links in their theoretical chain, Gibbs and Martin were able to conclude that the suicide rate of a population varies inversely with the degree of status integration.

Gibbs and Martin have tested their hypothesis against data on suicide rates in a variety of situations. Their measure of status integration was a simple one: the more people that belonged to a certain status category, the more highly integrated it was assumed to be. The results of the comparisons strongly supported Gibbs and Martin's hypothesis: the higher the status integration of a group, the lower the suicide rate, and vice versa. However, other sociologists have objected to the simple measure of status integration proposed by Gibbs and Martin, and few researchers have been motivated to explore the usefulness of this well-known reformulation of Durkheim's theory.

HENRY AND SHORT'S FRUSTRATION-AGGRESSION THEORY

One sociological theory of suicide has been founded on basic ideas other than Durkheim's. Andrew F. Henry and James F. Short (1954) based their theory on a psychological concept, the frustration-aggression hypothesis developed by Dollard and his colleagues (1939). This hypothesis suggests that aggressive behavior does not develop from an internal drive that needs satisfaction (such as hunger), but instead is produced when the environment frustrates people by blocking their approaches to a goal.

Henry and Short predicted that aggressive behaviors would occur in different patterns, depending on the extent to which the environment produced frustration. For example, they suggested that the business cycle should affect aggressive behavior because of the frustration it causes. They predicted (1) that suicide rates will rise during times of business depression and fall during times of business prosperity, while crimes of violence against others will rise during times of business prosperity and fall during times of business depression, and (2) that the effect of the business cycle on suicide rates will be greater for high- than for low-status groups, while the effect of the business cycle on homicide rates will be greater for low- than for high-status groups.

Henry and Short interpreted their results in terms of the frustration-aggression hypothesis. In order to do so, they made a number of assumptions. They assumed, first of all, that aggression is a consequence of frustration. Next they assumed that business cycles produce variations in the hierarchical rankings of persons by status. High-status persons lose rank relative to low-status persons during business contractions, while low-status persons lose relative rank during business expansions because they are less able to take advantage of the prosperity. They also assumed that frustrations are generated by a failure to maintain one's relative position in the status hierarchy. Finally, Henry and Short assumed that suicide occurs mainly in the high-status groups, and homicide mainly in the low-status groups.

With all these assumptions in mind, let us consider what happens to those who lose income during a business contraction. Higher-status people have more income to lose, and so their fall is greater than that of low-status people. High-status people lose rank relative to those of lower status, and low-status people may actually experience a relative gain in rank. Thus, in times of business contraction, frustration is generated in high-status people. Since they are prone to direct aggression inwardly, there is a rise in the suicide rate of high-status groups. There has been a great deal of research examining the association between suicide rates and the economy in the 40 years since Henry and Short's *Suicide and Homicide* was published, and while some of the studies support their theory, others do not.

Henry and Short speculated on other factors that might determine the direction in which aggression is expressed besides social class, factors such as the type and source of punishment given to children in a particular society and the degree of external social constraints on people's behavior. These aspects are discussed in other sections of this book.

OTHER THEORIES

A number of minor sociological theories of suicide have been proposed in recent years, and two merit mention here. The *critical-mass theory* is based on ideas developed by T.C. Schelling (1978). Schelling argued that when a behavior occurs in a society, it may at times increase to a critical frequency or mass beyond which so many people are showing the behavior that its incidence becomes self-sustaining. It then becomes a fashion or a fad. For example, the nations with the highest suicide rates in 1970 were also those that showed the greatest increase in suicide rates during the following decade (Lester, 1989), a result consistent with the critical-mass theory of suicide.

The *social deviancy theory* of suicide (Lester, 1989) is based on an idea proposed by Henry Wechsler and T.F. Pugh (1967), who argued that individuals who are deviant from the culture will experience greater stress, which in turn will increase their risk of psychiatric disorder. Thus people who are in a minority within a community should also have higher suicide rates. Although suicide rates of nonwhite Americans are lower than those of whites, research has found that the suicide rates of nonwhites are highest in those states where there are fewest nonwhites; similarly, the suicide rates of foreign immigrants to Australia vary inversely with the number of immigrants from a particular nation (Lester, 1989).

GENERAL COMMENTS

The sociological approach is a useful one in that it provides information about the relationships between social variables and suicide rates. However, sociological theories as a whole have left themselves open to a number of criticisms. It seems that a great deal of time has been spent trying to clarify Durkheim's theory, while the investment of energy could have been better employed in the development of new concepts. In addition to a tendency to make the interpretation of data fit preexisting assumptions, there have been biases of subject matter (for example, studying only completed suicide) that may have militated against the formation of sound theories. Sociologists have too readily accepted categories for subgroups provided by government agencies (such as whites and nonwhites), which do not make sense from a theoretical point of view, and they have often used official suicide statistics that may not be sufficiently reliable.

SUMMARY

Despite the foregoing criticisms, a great deal of knowledge has been accumulated about the suicide rates of societies. Durkheim's theory, proposed in the last century, remains the dominant theory in the field, and his classification of suicide into four types has been widely accepted and applied:

- egoistic suicide, where the individual's suicidal tendencies are not inhibited by strong social ties

- altruistic suicide, where people are so identified with a group that they sacrifice themselves for the good of the group

- fatalistic suicide, where society blocks realization of people's goals

- anomic suicide, where people are not constrained by the norms and values of their culture

Several more recent theorists have tried to reformulate Durkheim's ideas and make his theory a testable one. A theory of suicide based on the concept of status integration has been developed by Gibbs and Martin, who considered Durkheim's approach inadequate. Henry and Short proposed a sociological theory of suicide with a different basis, the Dollard frustration-aggression hypothesis. They believed that suicide results from frustration, and they examined the effects on suicidal behavior of the frustration generated by economic fluctuations.

REFERENCES

Dollard, J., Doob, L., Miller, N., et al. *Frustration and Aggression*. New Haven, CT: Yale University Press, 1939.

Douglas, J.D. *The Social Meanings of Suicide*. Princeton, NJ: Princeton University Press, 1967.

Durkheim, É. *Le Suicide*. Paris: Felix Alcan, 1897.

Durkheim, E. *Suicide*. Glencoe, IL: The Free Press, 1951.

Gibbs, J.P. Durkheim's heavy hand in the sociological study of suicide. In D. Lester (ed.), *Emile Durkheim: Le Suicide 100 Years Later*.
Philadelphia: The Charles Press, 1994.

Gibbs, J.P. and Martin, W.T. *Status Integration and Suicide*. Eugene:
University of Oregon Press, 1964.

Ginsberg, R.B. Anomie and aspirations. *Dissertation Abstracts*
27A:3945-3946, 1966.

Henry, A.F. and Short, J.F. *Suicide and Homicide*. New York: The Free
Press, 1954.

Johnson, B.D. Durkheim's one cause of suicide. *American Sociological
Review* 30:875-886, 1965.

Lester, D. *Suicide from a Sociological Perspective*. Springfield, IL:
Charles C Thomas, 1989.

Lester, D. (ed.). *Emile Durkheim: Le Suicide 100 Years Later*.
Philadelphia: The Charles Press, 1994.

Moksony, F. Ecological analysis of suicide. In D. Lester (ed.), *Current
Concepts of Suicide*. Philadelphia: The Charles Press, 1990.

Phillips, D.P., Ruth, T.E. and MacNamara, S. There are more things
in heaven and earth: missing features in Durkheim's theory of
suicide. In D. Lester (ed.), *Emile Durkheim: Le Suicide 100 Years
Later*. Philadelphia: The Charles Press, 1994.

Powell, E.H. Occupation status and suicide. *American Journal of
Sociology* 23:131-139, 1958.

Schelling, T.C. *Micromotives and Macrobehavior*. New York: W.W.
Norton, 1978.

Stack, S. The impact of divorce on suicide in Norway. *Journal of
Marriage and the Family* 51:229-238, 1989.

Taylor, S. Suicide, Durkheim and sociology. In D. Lester (ed.),
Current Concepts of Suicide. Philadelphia: The Charles Press, 1990.

Wechsler, H. and Pugh, T.F. Fit of individual and community characteristics and rates of psychiatric hospitalization. *American
Journal of Sociology* 73:331-338, 1967.

16

Drugs, Alcohol and
Suicidal Behavior

No cause-and-effect relationship has been established between suicide and the use of alcohol and/or drugs, but the consumption of these agents is often a contributing factor to suicide for several reasons. The use of alcohol and drugs may lower inhibitions and impair judgment of a person contemplating suicide and therefore make the act more likely, and alcohol and drug use aggravate other risk factors for suicide such as depression. Furthermore, because drugs are potentially lethal and relatively easy to obtain and use, they are often used as instruments of self-destruction. However, because it has been only relatively recently that large numbers of people have begun to use drugs to deliberately induce mood changes (as alcohol has been used for centuries), we do not have much information about how they relate to suicide. Perhaps this is due, in part, to the fact that people are typically more secretive about their drug use than they are about alcohol use. Moreover, different drugs have very different effects, and it may not be possible to draw conclusions that apply to all drugs.

One way in which drugs are thought to be different from alcohol, at least in the popular press, is that particular drugs are sometimes thought to *cause* suicide. For example, when Art Linkletter's daughter killed herself by jumping out of a window (allegedly, she thought she had the ability to fly), her father blamed her death on the LSD that she was high on and that she regularly used. After her death, Linkletter worked hard warning young people to stay away from the drugs that he felt killed his daughter. Linkletter's simplistic analysis, that attributed his daughter's suicide only to drug use, ignored her long history of disturbed behavior, including her very early and unhappy marriage.

In this chapter, I will examine the research findings about the effects of drugs and alcohol on suicidal behavior. As has been my practice in this book, I will not draw conclusions from single, incompletely reported cases like the one mentioned above, but instead will look at evidence gathered from large groups of suicidal people.

ALCOHOLISM, DRUG ABUSE AND SUICIDE

Alcoholism — genuine physical and psychological addiction to alcohol — was considered by Karl Menninger (1938) to be a form of suicidal behavior. The alcoholic way of life is clearly a self-destructive course. Real physiological damage can occur to the drinker's liver and brain. Jobs and social relationships are often destroyed, leaving the alcoholic with only the companionship of other heavy drinkers. Menninger called this type of behavior *chronic suicide* and saw it as motivated by the same self-destructive (though possibly unconscious) urges as suicide. Alternatively, suicide and alcoholism (and perhaps drug abuse as well) may be expressions of the same underlying causal variable, such as a history of social disorganization.

Substance abusers appear to have a higher incidence of both completed and attempted suicide than nonabusers (Lester, 1992). This may be because substance abuse has the following effects: it can disrupt social relationships and impair work performance, which leads to social isolation and social decline; it can increase impulsivity and lower restraints against self-harmful acts; it can increase self-deprecation and depressive tendencies that may increase the probability of suicidal behavior (Roy and Linnoila, 1986). Also, if a person is either a chronic alcoholic or acutely intoxicated, when he takes drugs, their effect can be much more lethal to the body.

DRUGS AS AN INSTRUMENT OF SUICIDE

Drugs are frequently used for committing suicide. From 1960 to 1980, the average suicide rate of 16 major nations of the world rose from 11.8 per 100,000 deaths per year to 14.8. The average rate of suicide for deaths that resulted from the ingestion of solid and liquid substances rose during this period from 2.3 to 3.0 (Lester, 1990). In the United States in 1980, the use of solid and liquid substances was the third most common method for suicide, after firearms and hanging (Baker et al. 1984) and in 1989, an analysis of 100,000 death found positive blood alcohol concentration (BAC) in 35 percent of suicide fatalities (National Committee for Injury Prevention and Control, 1993).

In developed nations, the majority of those using solid and liquid substances to commit suicide take them in the form of medications. (In developing nations, chemical fertilizers and insecticides are more commonly used.) Antidepressants are now the medications most frequently used for committing suicide, especially because physicians have become more cautious in prescribing barbiturates, once used in many suicidal deaths (Retterstol, 1993). However, the more recently developed antidepressants, such as Mianserin (a British drug), are much less likely to cause accidental and suicidal deaths than the older antidepressants, such as Elavil (amitriptyline) (Leonard, 1988).

There is good evidence that by making particular medications less available, it decreases the frequency of their use for suicide (Lester, 1993). For example, the use of barbiturates for suicide in the United States was directly associated with their sales volume (i.e., the more barbiturates were sold, the more they were used for suicide). Similarly, in 1961, in Japan, after laws were passed that made it necessary to have prescriptions to buy barbiturates and other sedatives, their use for suicide dropped.

Reflecting on these findings, Clarke and Lester (1989) have recommended the establishment of the following precautionary measures regarding potentially lethal medications: that doctors limit the number of pills in each prescription; that they prescribe the least toxic medications possible; that they not give automatic refills; that they never write prescriptions unless they have seen and evaluated the patient; that they prescribe suppositories rather than orally taken tablets; and that manufacturers enclose pills in plastic blisters as opposed to loose in a bottle so they are harder to get at, thereby limiting the ability to take large numbers at once. They have also called for the establishment of some sort of central state monitoring system that would detect instances in which people try to fill multiple prescriptions written by different physicians. It should also be able to detect forging and changing of prescriptions by patients.

DRUGS THAT INDUCE SUICIDE

From time to time, claims are made that a particular drug increases the risk of suicide. This claim has been made in the past about medications such as Valium (diazepam), LSD and Prozac (fluoxetine). Every now and then doctors who treat patients with these kinds of medications have a patient who commits suicide. They write a report that gets published in a scientific journal, and when other physicians read it, it encourages them to publish reports of their own similar experiences with medication and suicide. It is important to know, however, that in all cases where suicide has occurred as the result of prescribed medication, research that was based on thousands of individual patient studies did not show evidence that suicide is more common among patients who took the medication. In fact, a recent study found that Prozac is less often accompanied by suicidal behaviors than other antidepressants (Beasley et al., 1992).

DRUG AUTOMATISM

It is sometimes suggested that suicide by drug overdose can occur unintentionally. For example, after taking sleeping pills and falling into a partly conscious state, a person may forget that he has already taken pills and take more to achieve sleep or he may simply take more pills automatically, without being aware of the potentially lethal nature of what he is doing. This hypothetical state of action while being partially conscious has been called "automatism." Drug automatism has been suggested as a cause of occasional deaths through overdose, as in the case of the American writer Jack London, who died of a morphine overdose, a death that some commentators view as accidental and others view as suicidal.

Litman's group (1963) investigated incidents of apparent suicide caused by drugs and they found no evidence that drug automatism played a part in any of the deaths. In another investigation of 94 people who came close to death from drug overdose (Aitken and Proudfoot, 1963), 19 of the patients claimed that the overdose had been taken during an incident of drug automatism. However, after interviewing these people, the researchers concluded that in only two of the cases could the overdose conceivably have been due to automatism. Some of the patients completely denied having ingested drugs; these people tended to be older, to have more often used barbiturates, and to have gone into deeper comas than those who admitted taking drugs.

Perhaps the assumption that drug automatism *can* occur stems from the belief that suicide is a deliberate, voluntary act, that will always be remembered and admitted. However, we must not overlook the possibility that patients may lie about their suicide attempts. They may fear that if they admit their attempts, they will be ridiculed, scorned or punished. Even if they do not lie, it is possible that attempters will not remember their acts. Amnesia for the suicidal act can ensue from two causes. First, a physical trauma can easily result in retrograde amnesia — total loss of memory for a period preceding the injury. Somatogenic amnesia characteristically follows accidents in which a person receives a severe blow to the head, but it can also result from ingestion of barbiturates or alcohol and from attempted suicide by hanging (Stromgren, 1946). Second, amnesia may be psychogenic; that is, it may develop for psychological rather than physiological reasons. The memory of the suicidal act, and of the desperate mood associated with it, may be so distressing to individuals that it is repressed and cannot be recalled voluntarily. In such cases, the subjects are not lying, but honestly cannot remember what happened. But whether failure to report deliberate drug ingestion is due to lying, somatogenic amnesia or psychogenic amnesia, it is by no means clearly attributable to drug automatism.

ALCOHOL CONSUMPTION PRIOR TO SUICIDE

Alcohol can be involved with suicidal behavior in a number of ways. Used prior to suicide, alcohol can ease a person's fear of death and give him the courage to kill himself. It can be taken together with medications to increase the lethality of the drugs. Alternatively, people who have been drinking without serious suicidal intent might impulsively kill themselves while intoxicated.

It has been found that a significant proportion of completed and attempted suicides drink alcohol prior to their suicidal actions. Welte's group (1988) found that 33 percent of a sample of completed suicides from Erie County, New York, had alcohol in their bloodstream. In a British study, Varadaraj and Mendonca (1987) found that 41 percent of a sample of attempted suicides were intoxicated.

Alcohol intoxication at the time of the suicidal act is more common in those who leave no suicide note, have made no prior attempts, use a firearm and kill themselves in the evening or at night, and in males 20 to 60 years of age (Welte et al., 1988). Among suicide attempters, those who are intoxicated make more lethal attempts. It is conceivable that those engaging in suicidal behavior when intoxicated are more reckless and impulsive and therefore more likely to die.

SUMMARY

Because the use of alcohol and drugs is often associated with attempts to change unhappy moods, it is not surprising that they would be involved in suicidal behavior. Alcoholism and drug abuse are intrinsically self-destructive behaviors, and they are also associated with an increased risk of both completed and attempted suicide. Drugs, especially sedatives and antidepressants, are popular methods for suicide, and often despondent persons drink alcohol prior to their suicidal acts. Suicide in some cases has been attributed to a state known as "drug automatism" in which people overdose without serious suicidal intent, but there is little hard evidence for this phenomenon.

REFERENCES

Aitken, R.C. and Proudfoot, A.T. Barbiturate automatism. *Postgraduate Medicine* 45:612-616, 1963.

Baker, S.P., O'Neill, B. and Karpf, R.S. *The Injury Fact Book*. Lexington, MA: D.C. Heath, 1984.

Beasley, C.M., Potvin, J.H., Masica, D.N., et al. Fluoxetine. *Journal of Affective Disorders* 24:1-10, 1992.

Clarke, R.V. and Lester, D. Suicide: *Closing the Exits*. New York: Springer-Verlag, 1989.

Leonard, B.E. Cost benefit analysis of tricyclic antidepressant overdose. In B.E. Leonard and S.W. Parker (eds.), *Current Approaches: Risk/Benefits of Antidepressants*. Southampton, UK: Duphar Laboratories, 1988.

Lester, D. Changes in the methods used for suicide in 16 countries from 1960 to 1980. *Acta Psychiatrica Scandinavica* 81:260-261, 1990.

Lester, D. Alcoholism and drug abuse. In R.W. Maris, A.L. Berman, J.T. Maltsberger and R.I. Yufit (eds.), *Assessment and Prediction of Suicide*. New York: Guilford, 1992.

Lester, D. Controlling crime facilitators: Evidence from research on homicide and suicide. *Crime Prevention Studies* 1:35-54, 1993.

Litman, R.E., Shneidman, E.S., Farberow, N.L., et al. Investigations of equivocal suicides. *Journal of the American Medical Association* 184:924-929, 1963.

Menninger, K.A. *Man Against Himself*. New York: Harcourt, Brace & World, 1938.

National Committee for Injury Prevention and Control, "Injury Prevention: Meeting the Challenge," 1993.

Retterstol, N. *Suicide: A European Perspective*. New York: Cambridge University Press, 1993.

Roy, A. and Linnoila, M. Alcoholism and suicide. *Suicide and Life-Threatening Behavior* 16:244-273, 1986.

Stromgren, E. Mental sequelae of suicidal attempts by hanging. *Acta Psychiatrica* 21:753-780, 1946.

Varadaraj, R. and Mendonca, J. A survey of blood alcohol levels in self-poisoning cases. *Advances in Alcohol and Substance Abuse* 7(1):63-69, 1987.

Welte, J. Abel, E. and Wieczorek, W. The role of alcohol in suicides in Erie County, New York, 1972-1984. *Public Health Reports* 103:648-652, 1988.

17

Mental Illness and Suicide

When conducting a scientific investigation, one of the first things that must be done is to decide which questions are capable of being answered. Obviously, there is no point wasting time on questions that are unanswerable. A number of factors determine whether a question is answerable or not. First, if the question is stated in a meaningless way (for example, "What makes people tick?") and if it cannot be restated more meaningfully, then it cannot be answered. Second, there may be no way to determine the answer to the question from the available data. Third, the investigation of the act might change the process that would otherwise occur (for example, if a psychologist tries to measure a person's mental state before he pulled the trigger, it might also stop the person from pulling the trigger).

One of the most frequently asked questions about suicide — "Are suicidal people insane?" — risks being called unanswerable by all three of the criteria mentioned above. The question as it stands is not meaningful because the word "insane" has no precise meaning for behavioral scientists. (Lawyers may be willing to define it as a legal term, but psychologists, psychiatrists and sociologists are not.) Some psychologists would define mental illness as a state of abnormal biochemical functioning in the brain. Other psychologists would call it a behavior disorder resulting from maltreatment in childhood. Still others would say that mental illness is simply a learned behavior, a way of acting that people have chosen because at one time or another they were rewarded for it. Even if one were able to agree on a definition for the word "insane," it would still be difficult to determine whether the description were true of a particular suicidal person.

Asking the question "Are suicidal people insane?" leads to still other problems. One must decide whether the question means "Are they insane in general?" or "Are they insane for a brief period before the suicidal act?" The first way of interpreting the question gets us in trouble with the definition and measurement of "insanity." The second way of interpreting the question requires information that is almost impossible to obtain. Other people are rarely aware of the state of mind and behavior of suicidal people immediately before their acts. On occasion, suicides may talk into a tape recorder while they are dying, or may call a suicide prevention center shortly before death. However, this does not occur frequently enough for a general judgment to be made about the sanity of all suicidal people while they are in the process of committing suicide. Because we cannot answer the question "Are suicidal people insane?" suicidologists have turned to other relevant questions about mental illness and suicide.

SUICIDE RATES AMONG THE MENTALLY ILL

One approach to investigating mental illness in suicides is to interview friends and relatives of people who have completed suicide and to use their evidence in judging whether the behavior of the deceased, prior to committing suicide, was unusual. Estimates of the percentage of suicides who had a mental illness gathered by this method range from 5 to 94 percent — a range so large as to be practically meaningless (Lester, 1972). All of the higher estimates involved interviews with people who knew that the suicide had occurred, or were gathered by psychiatrists who firmly believe that all suicides are mentally ill; in both cases such factors could very well have biased their judgment. Psychiatrists who believe that the suicidal act is deranged would be more likely to conclude that any given suicide was mentally ill (see Robins, 1981). On the other hand, when objective data collected prior to the suicide are analyzed, the estimates of mental illness are much lower, ranging from about 5 to 22 percent (Lester, 1992). This evidence suggests that mental illness may be more common in suicidal than in nonsuicidal people and that a few suicides could very well have no mental illness.

Although no clinical definition exists for insanity, there are some characteristics related to mental illness that are easy to measure. One important question has to do with whether a person has been admitted to a mental hospital for treatment. A record of hospitalization generally indicates that a person has been behaving in some noticeably deviant fashion. Once people have been hospitalized, psychiatric records of their behavior problems are kept. The fact of hospitalization and the diagnostic record are two potentially useful pieces of data.

Early studies indicated that the suicide rate was higher among those who had been hospitalized for psychiatric reasons than among the rest of the population: 37.0 per 100,000 per year for those who had been hospitalized versus 9.6 for those who had not (Temoche et al., 1963). This general result has been replicated many times since the 1960s (for example, Evenson et al., 1982).

Determining the suicide rate for those hospitalized with different diagnoses is complicated by the meaning of the diagnosis. Each diagnostic category, like schizophrenia or major depressive disorder, is a label that includes a set of behaviors that tend to be found together. It is, most probably, not a label that identifies a single disease entity. Two cases of schizophrenia do not resemble each other in the way that two cases of measles or chickenpox do. Each schizophrenic's behavior is unique and has only a surface resemblance to another schizophrenic; moreover, two cases of schizophrenia may have different causal factors. Nonetheless it is customary to classify patients according to diagnosis, both as an aid in determining appropriate treatment and for research purposes.

Although the suicide rates reported for people with different diagnoses vary from study to study, there is rough agreement on the relative risks. Bipolar affective disorder (formerly known as manic-depressive psychosis) has the highest reported rate of completed suicide, while the anxiety, dissociation and conversion disorders (formerly known as neuroses) have the lowest rates. Pokorny (1964) reported the following suicide rates by diagnosis: depressive psychoses, 566 per 100,000 per year; schizophrenia, 167; organic disorders, 133; personality disorders, 130; neuroses and psychosomatic disorders, 119; and alcohol disorders, 78.

A review of recent research on this issue (Lester, 1992) concluded that affective disorders (both major depressive disorder and bipolar disorder) and schizophrenia are associated with a high rate of suicide, as is a diagnosis of substance abuse (both alcohol and drug abuse) and borderline personality disorder. A detailed analysis of studies on affective disorders (known as a meta-analysis) indicated that subsequent completed suicide was more common in patients diagnosed with unipolar affective disorder whereas subsequent attempted suicide was more common in patients diagnosed with bipolar affective disorder (Lester, 1992).

The high rate of completed suicide among those with depressive disorders is logical. Seriously depressed people see the world as a totally uninviting place. They believe that nothing will get better and there are few things that seem worth doing. (As we have noted in other chapters, this restriction of alternatives is typical of suicidal thinking.) Eventually, the boredom and weariness of remaining in a life where nothing is appealing may make the prospect of death and nothingness seem desirable. However, suicide rarely occurs in the depths of depression; it is much more likely to occur as the depression begins to lift. Perhaps it is only as people emerge from deepest depression that they have enough energy to act on their decision to choose death over life. Indeed, the risk of suicide for psychiatric patients is greatest in the three months after release from the hospital, when their depression has lessened and when they reencounter the stressors in life that contributed to their mental illness in the first place (Roy, 1982).

The role of depression in suicide is confirmed by several other areas of research. First, a depressed mood and in particular, the cognitive component of depression — feeling hopeless about the future — is one of the strongest predictors of suicide in all types of people (Beck et al., 1985). Second, research on the biochemistry of suicidal behavior, involving analyses of the urine, blood, cerebrospinal fluid and actual brain tissue of suicidal individuals, has confirmed that dysfunction in the serotonergic pathways is probably critical, and serotonin is the neurotransmitter implicated in the biochemical etiology of depression (Lester, 1988).

SPECIFIC SYMPTOMS AND SUICIDE

Although people with affective disorders (major depressive disorder and bipolar affective disorder) complete suicide more frequently, patients with other psychiatric diagnoses also kill themselves. An important question to ask is whether, within a diagnostic category, certain behavioral symptoms tend to accompany suicidal behavior. Is one kind of schizophrenic syndrome almost always accompanied by suicidal behavior, while others rarely are? Or do all types of schizophrenic patients have the same suicide rate? Suicidologists have tried to answer this question for a number of diagnostic categories, and not surprisingly, the presence of a formal secondary diagnosis of depression, or a high score on a measure of depressed mood, is usually the strongest predictor (see Drake et al., 1986).

Occasionally, one particular symptom seems to decrease or increase the risk of suicide. For example, Gittleson (1966) found that patients with a major depressive disorder who had obsessions (uncontrollable thoughts about a topic that recur repeatedly) had a lower incidence of suicidal behavior than those without obsessions (6 percent versus 38 percent). Perhaps these obsessions serve as a defense mechanism that protects the patients against suicide. The constant preoccupation with an obsessive idea may prevent the patient from having the time to think about suicide, or for that matter any other action. However, though this difference has been replicated (Kiev, 1974), it is not always found (Videbech, 1975).

SUICIDAL BEHAVIOR IN NEUROTICS AND PSYCHOTICS

"Neurosis" is a term once commonly used to categorize a group of psychiatric disorders characterized by high levels of anxiety. Unlike people with more severe psychiatric disorders (formerly known as "psychoses," that included schizophrenia and affective disorders), those with neuroses do not show the extreme deviance of behavior and thought that is found in psychotics. Even though they may think irrationally, they typically know that their thinking is irrational; nevertheless, they seem unable to control or change their thinking patterns. In the most recent revisions of the diagnostic system proposed by the American Psychiatric Association in 1993 and accepted by the federal government in 1994, these disorders have been reclassified according to whether they involve anxiety (anxiety disorders), amnesia (dissociative disorders), or muscular and sensory dysfunction (conversion disorders).

The problems that neurotics have can be sufficiently severe to keep them from fully enjoying life and performing at their maximum level. The differences between the two levels of psychiatric disturbance have led scholars to ask whether there are differences in the suicidal behavior of neurotics and psychotics.

It has been suggested that psychotics are more prone to complete suicide, while neurotics are more prone to attempt suicide. One early commentator thought that neurotics might play with the idea of suicide, but rarely with any determination (Gordon, 1929); their typical methods for suicide would be of quite low lethality. Karl Menninger (1938) agreed with this view, noting that neurotics may contemplate and even threaten suicide quite frequently, but rarely resort to serious suicidal behavior.

Although the relationship between the severity of psychiatric illness and the type of suicidal behavior has often been suggested, the hypothesis has not been extensively tested empirically. Dorpat and Boswell (1963) reported that more lethal suicidal attempts were made by psychotics, but Lester and Beck (1976) failed to find such a difference.

However, this association between neurosis/psychosis and the lethality of suicidal behavior might explain to some extent the gender difference in suicidal behavior discussed in Chapter 12. As noted in that chapter, there are strong gender differences in lethality of suicidal acts. Women tend to attempt suicide more often than men do, while men tend to complete suicide more often than women do. This gender difference in suicidal behavior might be attributable to a gender difference in the diagnosis of psychiatric disorders if such a difference existed. In fact, some surveys have reported gender differences in rates of psychiatric disorder, and when found, they often conform to the expected pattern. In one early survey, Roth and Luton (1943) found that more men than women were diagnosed as psychotic, and more women than men were diagnosed as neurotic.

More recently, in a study of five urban areas in the United States, Regier and associates (1988) found that men had a higher incidence of substance abuse (both alcohol and drug abuse) and antisocial personality disorder, whereas women had a higher incidence of affective, anxiety and somatization disorders (in which mental states are converted into bodily symptoms). These differences in the incidence of psychiatric disorders might well account for the continuing differences in suicidal behavior.

SUICIDES WITH DIFFERENT DIAGNOSES

It is feasible that people with different psychiatric disorders are motivated toward suicide for different reasons. In other words, there is no single stress or need that causes the suicides of all disturbed individuals. An event that precipitates suicide in those with one disorder may have little or no effect on those with a different disorder.

A study by Robins and O'Neal (1958) provides a good example of the differences that can exist in the suicidal behavior of different diagnostic groups. The researchers studied two groups of attempted suicides in a large general hospital. Group A had diagnoses of sociopathic personality, chronic alcoholism and conversion disorders (physical disabilities that occur in response to stress). Group B had bipolar affective disorder (manic-depressive psychosis) and chronic brain syndrome. People in Group A had suffered more broken homes as children, and as adults had more divorces, more arrests, more hospitalizations and more general social disruptions. All of the patients in Group A had at least one of these stressors in the six months prior to their suicide attempt, while less than half of the people in Group B had a recent experience of that kind. The people in Group A were more concerned with their feelings about others at the time of their suicide attempt, while those in Group B were more concerned with their feelings about themselves.

More recently, Lester, Beck and Steer (1989) compared a group of suicide attempters that were diagnosed with either antisocial personality disorder (psychopaths) or substance abuse disorder with a group of attempters diagnosed with depressive disorders. The two groups of attempters did not differ in the level of their depression or hopelessness. The depressive disorder attempters were more often female and married, were a little older and had made fewer prior suicide attempts. The depressive disorder attempters had greater suicidal intent in their suicidal actions, especially in respect to leaving a note and having expectations of dying as a result of their attempt.

Because psychiatric diagnosis is one of the most important characteristics to ascertain about a suicidal individual, much more research is needed to detail the particular kinds of suicidal actions made by those with different psychiatric diagnoses. The causal factors for suicidal behavior may differ for those with different diagnoses as will the appropriate treatment and their chances for subsequent suicidal preoccupation.

SUICIDE, SUGGESTIBILITY AND CONTAGION

The idea of a suicide "epidemic" stresses the role of imitation. Suicides do sometimes appear in clusters, and their acts as a group may resemble one another in method (Coleman, 1987). However, when Davidson and his colleagues investigated two clusters of suicide in teenagers who lived in Texas (Davidson et al., 1989), they found that those who imitated the first suicide had many other factors that could have prompted their suicide: they had been suicidal in the past, had recently experienced breakups with their boyfriends and girlfriends, had a record of arrests and were from broken homes. It seems unlikely that suicide can be "suggested" to someone who is free from stress and psychiatrically normal.

There has been a great deal of research into the claim that when television news and fictional dramas about suicides are aired, they are followed within days or weeks by an increase in the number of suicides (see Phillips and Carstensen, 1988), and the same is true of newspaper coverage of celebrity suicides (Stack, 1987). The suicide of Yukiko Okada illustrates this phenomenon. Yukiko, an 18-year-old singing idol in Japan, was distraught over her unhappy love affair with an actor. She was discovered in the morning of April 8, 1986 in a gas-filled apartment in Tokyo with her wrists slashed. Two hours later, she climbed to the roof of a seven-story recording studio and jumped to her death. In the next 17 days, 33 young people committed suicide, many of them jumping to their deaths as she did. On May 2, 21-year-old Masanno Majima jumped from the same roof as Yukiko and landed on the shrine that fans had erected to her memory. He had a photograph of Yukiko in his pocket.

Media Actions That Can Promote Suicide Contagion

Suicide researchers are in general agreement that the way in which the media treats the subject of suicide can have a marked effect on the incidence of imitative and cluster suicide and the development of a climate of contagion, especially among young people. The following is a list of media approaches that may be connected with increases in suicide among suggestible persons:

- Presenting simplistic explanations for suicide. This type of reporting does not acknowledge that most suicides are the result of a long personal history of psychosocial problems, a complex interaction of many factors. Oversimplified accounts can cause at-risk individuals to identify with the suicide based on only cursory similarities of situation.

- Repetitive or excessive reporting of suicide. Coverage that is given too much prominence is particularly compelling to suggestible adolescents and young adults. When coverage is sensationalized, the risk of inspiring a wave of suicide clusters is increased among persons who seize on the morbid details given in news reports. Dramatic photographs (such as the funeral, the site of the suicide and the victim's home) can be especially riveting to sensitive persons who might like to have similar attention after their own suicide.

- Reporting details of the suicide method. Technical descriptions of the method used and procedures followed in committing suicide may cause imitation of the suicidal behavior by self-destructive persons previously undecided about the particular course to take.

- Blurring the distinction between real and fictional suicides. Stories involving suicide presented in the form of television "docudramas" or "true-to-life" films can have an effect on a susceptible audience not unlike that of factual news accounts, except that their heightened dramatic character may, if anything, be even more compellingly suggestive, particularly to young people.

- Publicizing celebrity suicides. In an analysis of suicides from 1948 to 1983, Stack (1987) found that the publicized suicides of entertainers were associated with an increase of 217 suicides in the month of the publicity; these included reports on the deaths of film star Marilyn Monroe and television star Freddie Prinze. Stack found that reports on the suicides of political figures were associated with a more modest increase of 50 suicides in the month of publicity. Celebrities with strong followings (as opposed to celebrity-villains) can influence their most avid admirers even when they are dead.

- Presenting suicide as a reasonable solution to problems. Though most often an unintentional result, some accounts of suicide can make the act appear to some persons, particularly those looking for a rationale for their contemplated behavior, as a useful tool for problem-solving. Identification with an oversimplified account can cause some at-risk persons to see suicide as a possible coping mechanism.

- Emphasizing expressions of grief following a suicide. News coverage that reports at length on the outpourings of grief that were occasioned by a suicide may suggest to some people that society is honoring the suicidal behavior of the deceased, rather than simply mourning the death as a loss.

- Focusing disproportionately on the positive characteristics of the suicidal completer. Sympathy for the family and friends of the suicide often can result in background reporting that paints a very positive picture of the deceased without adequate attention to the troubles and problems of that person's life. When there is not enough balance in the reporting, suicidal behavior may appear attractive to some people, especially those who are not accustomed to receiving positive reinforcement.

All of the approaches discussed above have one thing in common: they can exercise an unwanted effect on persons who, for one reason or another, are abnormally sensitized to accounts of personal tragedy, in this case the tragedy of willful self-destruction. While we don't know very much about the extent to which imitation is a factor in suicide, some people feel very strongly that hearing about suicide will cause susceptible people to copy the behavior. Perhaps if the media was aware of the potential effects of sensationalized reporting and they presented their reports of suicide accordingly, the chances of media reporting increasing the risk of suicide could be reduced.

SUMMARY

It is not possible to answer the seemingly simple question, "Are suicidal people insane?" However, we can answer other questions that have direct or indirect bearing on the relationship between mental illness and suicide. The suicide rate is higher among those who have been hospitalized for mental illness, and it is highest among patients who have been diagnosed with an affective disorder (severe depression with or without mania). For some diagnostic categories, it is possible to find symptoms that accompany suicidal behavior, but research has not systematically explored predictors of suicide in all of the major diagnostic categories. There is evidence that imitation and suggestion can play a role in precipitating suicidal behavior, but it appears likely that this may occur only in those who are psychiatrically disturbed and already suicidal.

REFERENCES

Beck, A.T., Steer, R.A., Kovacs, M. and Garrison, B. Hopelessness and eventual suicide. *American Journal of Psychiatry* 142:559-563, 1985.

Coleman, L. *Suicide Clusters*. Boston: Faber & Faber, 1987.

Davidson, L.E., Rosenberg, M.L., Mercy, J.A., et al. An epidemiological study of risk factors in two teenage suicide clusters. *Journal of the American Medical Association* 262:2687-2692, 1989.

Dorpat, T. and Boswell, J.W. An evaluation of suicidal intent in suicide attempts. *Comprehensive Psychiatry* 4:117-125, 1963.

Drake, R.E., Gates, C. and Cotton, P. Suicide among schizophrenics. *British Journal of Psychiatry* 149:784-787, 1986.

Evenson, R.C., Wood, J., Nuttall, E. and Cho, D. Suicide rates among public mental health patients. *Acta Psychiatrica Scandinavica* 66:254-264, 1982.

Gittleson, N.L. The relationship between obsessions and suicidal attempts in depressive psychoses. *British Journal of Psychiatry* 112:889-890, 1966.

Gordon, R.G. Certain personality problems in relation to mental illness with special reference to suicide and homicide. *British Journal of Medical Psychology* 9:60-66, 1929.

Kiev, A. Prognostic factors in attempted suicide. *American Journal of Psychiatry* 131:987-990, 1974.

Lester, D. *Why People Kill Themselves*, Ed. 1. Springfield, IL: Charles C Thomas, 1972.

Lester, D. *The Biochemical Basis of Suicide*. Springfield, IL: Charles C Thomas, 1988.

Lester, D. *Why People Kill Themselves*, Ed. 3. Springfield, IL: Charles C Thomas, 1992.

Lester, D. Suicidal behavior in bipolar and unipolar affective disorders. *Journal of Affective Disorders* 27:117-121, 1993.

Lester, D. and Beck, A.T. Suicidal behavior in neurotics and psychotics. *Psychological Reports* 39:549-550, 1976.

Lester, D., Beck, A.T. and Steer, R.A. Attempted suicide in those with personality disorders. *European Archives of Psychiatry and Neurological Sciences* 239:109-112, 1989.

Menninger, K. *Man Against Himself.* New York: Harcourt, Brace & World, 1938.

Phillips, D.P. and Carstensen, L.L. The effect of suicide stories on various demographic groups. *Suicide and Life-Threatening Behavior* 18:100-114, 1988.

Pokorny, A.D. Suicide rates in various psychiatric disorders. *Journal of Nervous and Mental Disease* 139:499-506, 1964.

Regier, D.A., Boyd, J.H., Burke, J.D., et al. One-month prevalence of mental disorders in the United States. *Archives of General Psychiatry* 45:977-986, 1988.

Robins, E. *The Final Months.* New York: Oxford University Press, 1981.

Robins, E. and O'Neal, P. Culture and mental disorder. *Human Organization* 16(4):7-11, 1958.

Roth, W.F. and Luton, F.H. The mental health program in Tennessee. *American Journal of Psychiatry* 99:662-675, 1943.

Roy, A. Risk factors for suicide in psychiatric patients. *Archives of General Psychiatry* 39:1089-1095, 1982.

Stack, S. Celebrities and suicide. *American Sociological Review* 52:401-412, 1987.

Temoche, A., Pugh, T.F. and MacMahon, B. Suicide rates among current and former mental institution patients. *Journal of Nervous and Mental Disease* 138:124-130, 1963.

Videbech, T. The psychopathology of anancastic endogenous depression. *Acta Psychiatrica Scandinavica* 52:336-373, 1975.

18

Time, Season, Weather
and Suicide

Naive theories often assert that suicide is more likely to occur at certain times or when certain weather conditions exist. Various times, some of them mutually exclusive, are thought to be especially likely occasions for suicide, such as Christmas or other holidays, winter, spring and the anniversaries of loved ones' deaths. It is believed that suicide is more likely to occur at night than during the day. Weather conditions, too, are seen as creating an atmosphere conducive to for suicide; bad weather is seen as depressing, while the high suicide rate in California has led people to implicate good weather as well. Suicidologist Arnold Stoper has theorized (in a personal conversation with the author) that during bad weather people blame their depression on the weather, and when good weather comes they lose their excuse. This inability to externalize blame increases the chance that they will kill themselves. He attributes the high suicide rate in California to the fact that bad weather is rare, therefore people cannot often blame their depression on external sources such as the weather, so they turn it inward with the act of suicide.

In recent years, suicidologists have tried to test the many possibilities for relationships between the occurrence of suicides and temporal or meteorological variables. Let us examine some of the work that has been done.

SEASONAL RHYTHMS

It has long been recognized that there is a seasonal variation in the rate of completed suicide. In his general overview, Louis Dublin (1963) noted that between 1910 and 1923 the variation was quite clear. The peak number of suicides occurred in May, with the rate then falling month by month to its low in December, a difference that was statistically significant. The seasonal variation was more marked in rural than in urban areas. More recently, according to Dublin's investigations, the pattern has changed. The peak is still in April or May and the low point in December, but the variation is less clear than it was, and there are subsidiary peaks. Perhaps this change is related to the effects of increasing urbanization.

If the suicide rate really does follow a seasonal trend, there should be a reverse pattern in the Southern Hemisphere from that in the Northern Hemisphere. Dublin investigated seasonal variation in Australian suicide rates for three separate years, but found little consistency in peaks and troughs. Other researchers have reported a peak during the Australian spring (September and October), but their results were not statistically significant (Edwards and Whitlock, 1968). More recent evidence (Lester, 1979; Bollen, 1983) indicates that the major peak for suicide in the United States is between April and May with a secondary peak between August and October, though this secondary peak may exist only for women.

It remains unclear just why there is a seasonal variation in suicide rates. Perhaps there is a seasonal variation for deaths of all kinds, and suicide does not have any special relationship to the seasons (although Lester's 1979 study did not find a spring peak for homicidal deaths). Emile Durkheim (1897) suggested that the seasonal variation might be due to differences in social activity during the different seasons, but it is premature to evaluate this hypothesis because no data relevant has yet been collected.

HOLIDAYS

Some people believe that the suicide rates are high on major holidays because they imagine that lonely people feel left out of celebrations, or, alternatively, that there are low rates on holidays because potential suicides are too busy with holiday activities to think about suicide. Lester (1979) and Phillips and Wills (1987) found that suicide rates are lower on the six major national holidays in the United States (New Year's Day, Memorial Day, Independence Day, Labor Day, Thanksgiving and Christmas Day).

In an extensive study of the possible association between astrology and suicide rates in New York, Press (1978) found no differences between the sample and people who died of natural causes. Furthermore, of 18 astrologers surveyed, only one could identify suicides from their astrological charts at a level better than chance.

DAY OF THE WEEK

Intuition suggests that some days of the week are more likely to have high suicide rates than others. "Blue" Monday, when people must return to work or to school after the weekend, might be considered an especially dangerous day. Indeed, Lester's (1979) and Bollen's (1983) studies on United States data confirmed that Monday is the most popular day for suicide. (This Monday peak appears to be stronger for men than for women and stronger for adults than for teenagers.)

TIME OF DAY

As noted earlier, night is often thought of as the principal time when suicide occurs. This assumption is supported by the importance that suicide prevention centers typically place on 24-hour availability. However, in a study of completed suicides in Los Angeles County in 1957, Shneidman and Farberow (1961) found that significantly more suicides occurred between noon and 6 p.m., and significantly fewer between midnight and 6 a.m. This general result has been found in more recent studies, albeit of smaller samples (Lester, 1992).

WEATHER

Early work on the relationship between weather and suicide rates concentrated largely on finding logical reasons for the hypothesized associations rather than on empirically investigating whether the association exists. In 1909, Phillips posited that hot, humid and windy weather causes extensive low-grade skin irritation, making the nervous system more irritable and therefore increasing the likelihood of suicide. Phillips suggested that the annual variation in the quality and quantity of foods that people eat might lead to an association between the suicide rate and the weather. Hopkins (1937) later argued that social activity varied with the weather and was responsible for any relation between the weather and the suicide rate. Still, it remained hard to say whether there should be more social activity during bad weather (when many people stay at home) or during good weather (when they tend to go out).

It was only in the 1960s that empirical investigations of the association between the weather and the suicide rate were conducted. Much of the work was done by Pokorny and his associates in Houston, Texas (Pokorny, 1964, 1966a, 1966b; Pokorny, Davis and Harberson, 1963). They examined the relationships between rates of completed suicide and of attempted suicide and 11 weather variables (temperature, wind speed, wind direction, barometric pressure, relative humidity, visibility, ceiling height, rain, fog, thunderstorms and cloudiness). When the data were controlled for the differences in the frequency of weather conditions in the course of a year, no significant relationships were found between any of the variables and the rates of either attempted or completed suicide. Furthermore, passage of a cold front was not associated with any change in the incidence of suicide, either on the day of passage or on the days before and after. Research conducted since Pokorny's time generally supports this lack of an association (Lester, 1992).

THE MOON AND THE SUN

It has long been believed that there is a relationship between the moon and behavioral disturbances. Severe emotional disturbances have been attributed to the influence of the moon to such an extent that the word lunacy is derived from the Latin word for moon. Werewolves were thought to change from human to wolf under the influence of the full moon. A person who is vague and unalert may be called "moonstruck." With all of these folk beliefs about the power of the moon, it was inevitable that suicidologists would investigate the relationship between moon phase and suicide. Pokorny (1964) studied all completed suicides in Texas during a three-year period, and noted the phase of the moon and the point on the apogee-perigee cycle for each suicide. He found no significant relations for the whole sample of suicides or for subgroups by age and gender.

Although occasional studies on small samples have documented an association between the phase of the moon and suicidal behavior (for example, Jones and Jones, 1977), research with larger samples, such as for the whole United States (Lester, 1979; MacMahon, 1983), has not confirmed such a link.

Pokorny (1966b) also investigated the relationship between sunspot activity and the rate of suicide, but found no correlation even when he allowed for a possible lag of several days between sunspots and the suicidal act.

SUMMARY

Studies involving possible associations of time, season and weather have yielded little new knowledge about suicide. Even though a seasonal variation does exist, as does a relationship to day of the week and time of day, weather, sunspots and the phase of the moon do not seem to have a bearing on the suicide rate.

REFERENCES

Blachley, P.H. and Fairley, N. Market analysis for suicide prevention. *Northwest Medicine* 68:232-238, 1969.

Bollen, K. Temporal variations in mortality. *Demography* 29:45-49, 1983.

Dublin, L. *Suicide*. New York: Ronald Press, 1963.

Durkheim, E. *Le Suicide*. Paris: Felix Alcan, 1897.

Edwards, J.E. and Whitlock, F.A. Suicide and attempted suicide in Brisbane. *Medical Journal of Australia* 1:932-938, 1968.

Hopkins, F. Attempted suicide. *Journal of Mental Science* 83:71-94, 1937.

Jones, P.K. and Jones, S.L. Lunar association with suicide. *Suicide and Life-Threatening Behavior* 7:31-39, 1977.

Lester, D. Temporal variation in suicide and homicide. *American Journal of Epidemiology* 109:517-520, 1979.

Lester, D. *Why People Kill Themselves*. Springfield, IL: Charles C Thomas, 1992.

MacMahon, K. Short-term temporal cycles in the frequency of suicide. *American Journal of Epidemiology* 117:744-750, 1983.

Phillips, D.P. and Wills, J.S. A drop in suicides around national holidays. *Suicide and Life-Threatening Behavior* 17:1-12, 1987.

Phillips, W. Seasonal influences on suicide. *Transactions of the American Clinical Climatological Association* 25:156-166, 1909.

Pokorny, A.D. Moon phases, suicide and homicide. *American Journal of Psychiatry* 121:66-67, 1964.

Pokorny, A.D. Suicide and weather. *Archives of Environmental Health* 13:255-256, 1966a.

Pokorny, A.D. Sunspots, suicide and homicide. *Diseases of the Nervous System* 27:347-348, 1966b.

Pokorny, A.D., Davis, F. and Harberson, W. Suicide, suicide attempts and weather. *American Journal of Psychiatry* 120:377-381, 1963.

Press, N. The New York suicide study. *Journal of Geocosmic Research* 2(2):23-33, 1978.

Shneidman, E.S. and Farberow, N.L. Statistical comparisons between committed and attempted suicides. In N.L. Farberow and E. S. Shneidman (eds.), *The Cry for Help*. New York: McGraw-Hill, 1961.

19

An Individual Case of Suicide

Although we cannot draw conclusions about suicides in general from the examination of one individual case of suicide, we can learn a good deal by analyzing such a case. Readers who are new to the study of suicidal behavior may find the statistical content of research dry and difficult to associate with actual people. For this reason, I think it would be beneficial to present a psychological autopsy of a single suicide. A psychological autopsy (Weisman and Kastenbaum, 1968) is not simply a case report; it is a research method for determining the psychological processes that may have contributed to a person's suicide. A lot of information that is not specifically relevant to the dynamics of an individual suicide may find its way into a medical examiner's report, but unlike a case report, the psychological autopsy is directed primarily toward the emotional processes that moved the person toward his death. Information about these processes is gathered through extensive interviews with friends and relatives. In my psychological autopsy of Thomas McCleary, I will report the information given by those who had known the deceased, and then analyze some of the details in the case by applying the research findings discussed earlier in this book.*

THE SUICIDE OF THOMAS McCLEARY

At the age of 31, Thomas McCleary killed himself by cutting his throat and bleeding to death. Information about his life and his activities just before his suicide was obtained through interviews with his girlfriend, his mother and a close male friend.

---

* I would like to thank Dr. Gene Brockopp for allowing me to use this case material. Real names and other identifying information have been changed to ensure privacy.

Statement of Tom's Girlfriend, Christine Blaszkopanick

Christine Blaszkopanick was a 28-year-old mother of Polish extraction who had been divorced several times. Her two children lived in foster homes. She was an attractive woman, but she was slightly overweight. She was once hospitalized briefly for an emotional disturbance. Her vocabulary and use of language indicated above-average intelligence, but her responses showed little emotion. Christine and Tom met in a bar and almost immediately began to live together. At the time of the interview, Christine was four months pregnant with Tom's child. They had planned to get married in December (about two weeks after his suicide).

When Christine was asked to describe Tom's personality, she emphasized that he was insecure and that he tried to keep his tensions under control by using drugs and alcohol. His insecurity seemed to be based on issues, stemming from his childhood: that he felt different from most of the people he knew because he had not been baptized; that because of divorce his father was not there for him; that he could never trust anyone because he had not been able to trust his father. Christine said that Tom liked to question her about her past and then respond with negative remarks. However, most of the time when they were alone together, Christine described Tom as "warm, gentle, understanding, sensitive, kind and intelligent." In contrast, when they were with other people, Tom was cold, distant and critical of Christine. He reacted rudely or with dislike if he perceived that other people were acting insincerely or if he felt they were superior to him.

Christine believed that Tom constantly struggled with inner conflicts and tensions. He usually managed to keep these feelings under control, but sometimes they would surface in his anxieties, depressions, physical twitches and violent behavior. At times his hands would twitch or become immobile and his facial muscles would go into spasms. When this happened, Tom would get a drink or take some pills. He was constantly drinking beer and smoking. At times, he would be violent; he said he could kill someone if he had to. When Tom and Christine had a disagreement, he wouldn't hesitate to hit her. Afterward he would apologize and beg her not to leave him. (She often did leave after they quarreled, but she always returned in a day or two.)

According to Christine, Tom had only a few friends; "he could not stand people and would deliberately drive them away." The only long-term friend he had was George Adams, whose statement about Tom follows. When Christine was asked about Tom and

George's relationship, she became very agitated and said she would only talk about it if she was assured that George would never see her statement. When the interviewer quelled her fears, she stated that even though Tom had not really liked George, he had always been there when Tom needed him. George was apparently attracted to Tom, she added, but they did not have a sexual relationship. However, Tom had told her that before she came to live with him, on two different occasions, both times when he was drunk, George had tried to "fondle" him. On a number of occasions, she said, George had taken off all his clothes in front of Tom. Once Christine had hidden in the closet when George came to see Tom and she heard George say that he liked to go to the gym and look at other men's bodies. She had asked George to stop seeing Tom for a few months, but George claimed that Tom needed him. George had become very angry when he learned that Christine and Tom were going to get married. He had been supporting both of them financially. (Later, at Tom's funeral, George told Christine that he did not intend to go on helping her.)

Christine said that as far as she knew, Tom had not made any suicide threats or attempts during the time they were living together. She recalled that a few weeks before his death, Tom had said that if a person really wanted to kill someone, it would not be hard: "just go from here to here with a razor," he had said, drawing his finger across his neck from ear to ear.

Describing the events that led up to Tom's suicide, Christine said that one Sunday in November, he had begun drinking vodka heavily and had continued to drink throughout the next week. He was also taking amphetamines. He continued drinking and taking pills until he was unconscious and as soon as he woke up, he began again. He also pawned many of his possessions to get money to drink, and talked about robbing a liquor store. He kept saying he would "taper off tomorrow," but never did so. Christine said that on Tuesday she told him she could not take it any more and left, but she decided to return the following day and stayed until Friday. On Wednesday, Tom started putting cigarettes out by pressing them against his body. He told Christine, "I would ask you to do it to me but I know you wouldn't do it." On Friday, Christine said that she told Tom that she could not marry him "as he was," and left again. She said that Tom did not respond particularly emotionally to this statement, and walked her downstairs, "acting kind of goofy" and talking about a gun. She returned later that night and found that he had chained the door closed. This disturbed Christine because Tom had told her that the only time he ever chained the door was when he was afraid that someone was after him or that he might hurt someone else. After letting Christine in, Tom went out to buy more liquor. Even though Christine had told him she would wait for his return, she decided to leave. On Saturday, Tom was looking for Christine and when he ran into George Adams, told him that he thought she had left him for good. On Sunday, Christine called Adams and was told that Tom had killed himself.

Statement of Tom's Friend, George Adams

George Adams was a self-employed architect. A self-assured and soft-spoken man, he appeared to be a devoted husband and father and was active in church work.

George and Tom McCleary met about five years before Tom committed suicide in a chance encounter on the street. George was on his way to a local men's club. A few days later he ran into Tom again. It was raining, so George offered to share his umbrella; this was the beginning of their friendship.

George said that they became friends because he liked Tom's personality. Tom was "commanding, he dressed well, he was an outstanding individual, he had a spectacular personality, physical beauty, and a way of handling himself." George believed that he was Tom's only friend and that Tom didn't have other friends because "he took advantage of anyone he came in contact with." Although George realized that he, too, was perhaps being taken advantage of, he did not resent it. Instead, he said he regarded Tom "as my son, as a problem child." (Mrs. Adams interrupted her husband at this point in the conversation to say of Tom that she "hated his guts.")

In keeping with George's paternal feelings toward Tom, he was concerned with the fact that Tom "never really had a chance" because of his family's confused home life, which left the boy on his own from the age of 12 or 13. George wanted to give Tom a better sense of values, because he thought Tom had such "great potential, such a magnetic personality, and was so very charming." According to George, Tom "rejected all things of a constructive nature...[he] indulged himself in whatever he wanted to do...he lived only for the moment." Tom was always "full of wild threats" and "spoke of being dead before he was 30." George said that he "pooh-poohed the idea." In spite of these quirks, "Tom made an outstanding appearance in any group" and inspired such regard in George that he became Tom's "sole source of income...I paid the landlord, bought him food, took him out to eat, but rarely gave him money."

George became involved in Tom's relationships with his family members and learned a good deal about them. On two occasions he not only paid for Tom's mother to come visit from Arkansas, but he also invited her to stay with him and his family. On at least one occasion, he took Tom to Arkansas to visit Tom's mother. George said that Tom loved his mother, who was a "competent and intelligent woman" employed as a draftsman. Tom's father, on the other hand, was the object of Tom's hatred because he had abused and rejected him during his boyhood. Tom spoke little of his older sister, but was proud of his younger brother, who was studying for an advanced degree.

George also involved himself in Tom's relationships with women. He hired a lawyer on Tom's behalf in order to start divorce proceedings against Tom's wife, but did not think that Tom ever went through with the suit.

During the five years that George knew him, Tom was involved in a number of escapades. In most of the cases, George offered support, paid fines and did whatever else he could to help. Tom was jailed for drunkenness, as well as for armed assault and robbery. He was hospitalized several times and attempted suicide on one of those occasions.

George was in close contact with Tom during the week prior to his death. Tom seemed depressed and George said that he attributed this to Christine's abrupt departure and to the pressure he was putting on Tom to deal with his alcoholism by going into the hospital. George also believed that the Thanksgiving holiday was difficult for Tom because he was "alone without food or money and...drinking heavily." George managed to get Tom to make a brief visit to an alcoholism clinic on the day before Thanksgiving, when Tom was "in bad shape and incoherent."

On the following Saturday night, Tom called George to ask to be taken to the hospital. When George returned the call a little later to make sure Tom was still willing to go, he found that Tom had changed his mind. Three calls came from Tom in the next four hours. During the last call, Tom told George, "I want to see you and be with you," but because Tom still refused to go to the hospital, George did not agree to visit him. At 8:30 the next morning, George went to Tom's apartment to check on him. Tom said that he felt awful and was ready to go to the hospital; he was lying in bed, fully dressed, but unshaven and puffy-faced.

The two went by car to a well-known private hospital, but when they got there, Tom said, "I'm not going in. I'm afraid. They won't take me here." George agreed that they probably would not admit

Tom, and asked where he wanted to go. Tom named a nearby state hospital and said he would cooperate if he was taken there. But once they arrived at the hospital, Tom again refused to go in, saying that he was afraid. George acquiesced, telling Tom, "I can understand that, it would have been painful...I won't force you."

By this time it was late morning, and George wanted to go to church, so he took Tom back to his apartment. Tom asked him not to leave, then to buy him a drink. George refused to get Tom a drink, but agreed to stay for a few minutes. When George finally left, Tom asked whether he would come back, and George said he would return around 3 o'clock.

At that time, George came back with some sandwiches for Tom and used his key to get in. He noticed blood on the bed and then found Tom's dead body in the bathroom.

Statement of Tom's Mother, Millicent McCleary

Tom's mother looked younger than her age. She dressed conservatively. She was quiet and controlled as she talked about Tom in a detached voice. Only toward the end of the interview did she show any emotion.

Mrs. McCleary was divorced and remarried to the same man three times. The divorces occurred when Tom was between the ages of 7 and 14. Tom's father, Steven, was a writer. The mother described him as an alcoholic and a man who "didn't want a family." Tom had two siblings: a slightly older sister and a brother five and a half years younger.

Mrs. McCleary remembered Tom as a large, healthy baby whose early development was normal. She added, however, that Tom became a solemn child who usually played by himself. Only at the age of 10 or 11 did he begin to "go to the end of the block and play with other boys." This didn't work out, she said, because he was a poor loser at games. Although Mrs. McCleary was told that Tom had a high intelligence test score, he was expelled from every school he attended. In the tenth grade, he was barely passing.

Tom's relationship with his father during this period was very poor. Mr. McCleary "was always picking at him and asking embarrassing questions." Tom's mother felt that a "father is always jealous of his older son." She vividly recalled an incident between 13-year-old Tom and his father. "His father was drunk and Tom pinned him against the corner of the wall and beat his face until it was unrecognizable...this is where Tom tore everything down...he could never look up to his father again."

When Tom was 14, he was sent to a reformatory for 13 months. According to his mother, no specific charges were filed against him, but he would "roam in the streets until 2 a.m." She added that he "hid guns" and was "accused of street fighting."

When Tom was 15, Mrs. McCleary took him to a psychiatrist for treatment. He left school during that year. He also shot himself in the stomach with a rifle and had to have his spleen removed. He later let his mother know it was a deliberate act. After he recovered, he had several jobs with local businesses.

Tom joined the U.S. Army at the age of 17 with his mother's permission. He received an honorable discharge after two years. Mrs. McCleary felt that Tom liked army life and seemed to do well during this time. Upon leaving the service, he went to live with his former psychiatrist for a year, and then got his own apartment. (Although Mrs. McCleary approved of Tom's military experience, she seemed resentful and anxious about his relationship with the psychiatrist.)

Tom got married in his early twenties and had two children. Mrs. McCleary was under the impression that the couple were divorced two years before Tom's death. She never saw her daughter-in-law or grandchildren, although she frequently talked to Tom on the telephone.

Mrs. McCleary last saw Tom two years before his death, when he visited her at home. She felt at the time that he had changed. He did not want to be seen with his brother for fear that he might embarrass him and his friends. She recalled that Tom was drinking heavily and on two occasions had crushed a glass in his bare hands.

Looking back over Tom's adulthood, Mrs. McCleary noted that he "didn't get along with anyone very well; he had no friends over a year or two except Mr. Adams." She thought that the friendship was maintained only because of George Adams' patience and the special effort he made. She said of Tom that "he had everything — looks, brains, talent," that "he was afraid to let anyone close to him," that "he was a complex person" who in some ways "almost quit growing somewhere back there." Mrs. McCleary frequently referred to her son as "poor little Tom — he will always be my little boy."

The last time Mrs. McCleary talked to Tom was about two weeks before his death. He called to introduce her to Christine, to tell her about his plans for getting married, and to ask for $300 so he could travel to Arkansas. Although she had given him money before, she refused this time. She thought he had been drinking heavily at the time of the telephone call.

In talking about Tom's suicide, his mother said that because "he was afraid to let anyone get close to him," he must have felt that "there was no use staying around...that it's going to end some day, so let's end it now." She became angry and said that she could understand homicide but could not understand someone who wanted to die. She was not planning to tell Tom's brother and sister that he had committed suicide. She would just say he got his "pills and alcohol mixed; no one will know for sure." It seemed to the interviewer that she was trying to protect both herself and Tom's memory from the intrusions of reality.

COMMENTS

Like every individual case of completed suicide, Tom McCleary's has unique qualities. While, of course, Tom was his own person and cannot be expected to display all of the possible characteristics of suicides, when we examine the case, we must conclude that Tom shared a number of characteristics with suicides as a group.

Family Background and Relationships

Like many other completed suicides, Tom McCleary came from a highly unstable family. His parents' three divorces and remarriages created a constantly changing home life. When the parents were together, the father's alcoholism and aloofness destroyed any chance for a good relationship between him and Tom. The two relatively decent relationships that Tom had with members of his family were also distant ones. He was fond of his younger brother, but in later years refused to be seen with him for fear of embarrassing him — an indication that the relationship was not a secure one. He maintained contact with his mother and said that he loved her, but she never even met his wife or children.

Social Relationships

All of the interviewees confirmed that Tom had few friends and that the friendships he developed were usually brief. His relationship with Christine does not appear to have been a deeply intimate one, beginning as it did with a casual pickup and developing apparently into a drinking companionship. The friendship with George was maintained primarily through George's own efforts. George's motivation for keeping up the relationship is not clear; if Christine's statements are true, homosexual elements as well as altruistic ones were involved. In any case, based on known facts, the friendship was not a matter of mutual affection and support.

Previous Suicidal Acts

As was noted earlier, the personal history of a completed suicide often shows previous suicidal acts, suicide threats and other forms of self-destructive behavior. The statements of Tom McCleary's friends and relatives show that Tom behaved in these ways from an early age. Recalling his teenage years, his mother mentioned his self-inflicted stomach wound. George Adams informed the interviewer that Tom had attempted suicide during one of his periods of hospitalization. Several weeks before he took his life, Tom had described to Christine how easy it would be to kill a person by cutting his throat (the very method he used on himself).

Emotional Disturbance

Tom first received psychiatric treatment in his teens. As an adult, he was hospitalized several times and became sufficiently familiar with the local mental health system to know which hospitals would accept him and which would not.

Loss of Social Relationships

Tom's early life was marked by his father's repeated absences through divorce. Even when Mr. McCleary was present, his aloofness and heavy drinking made the family virtually fatherless. Later, divorce separated Tom from his wife and children, leaving him relatively isolated, because the friendships and relationships he had with his family were not sufficiently close. The pattern of loss culminated at a crucial time with the departure of Christine, an event that probably played an important role in triggering Tom's suicide. Although Christine claimed that Tom should have known she would return, George's statement indicated that Tom was convinced she had gone for good.

George's Complicity

The people who are close to a suicidal individual may actually cooperate with him in bringing about his death. George Adams seems to have played such a role in Tom's suicide. Perhaps the clearest evidence for this lies in George's description of his visits with Tom to hospitals just before the suicide. It must have been obvious that Tom was in a highly disturbed state, and that he wished to be hospitalized even though he was scared to do it. Although he was aware of Tom's previous hospitalizations and of one suicide attempt, George did not encourage Tom to go to the hospital. He agreed to take him when Tom asked, but then cast doubt on Tom's decision to go by telephoning to ask if he had changed his mind. When Tom finally asked to be driven to a hospital, George, according to his own account, did not urge him to go in. On the contrary, he agreed with Tom's negative statements about the hospitals — that the first probably would not admit him and that it would be very painful to go into the second. (This behavior, in addition to George's earlier refusal to visit Tom unless he agreed to go to the hospital, seems to indicate a double-binding tendency that may have been characteristic of the relationship.) When the two returned to Tom's apartment, George refused to miss church in order to comply with Tom's urgent request for him to stay, although he had previously made many sacrifices of time and money for Tom.

Considering that George's behavior could have been an encouragement for Tom's suicide, we may ask what possible advantage Tom's death would have had for George. Christine's statement about George's homosexual interest, if true, could be the key here. George's involvement with Tom was deep in terms of the responsibility he had taken on. This could have been rewarding in sexual terms, for it brought the two men into close contact. On the other hand, the relationship must have caused trouble for George at home. His wife disliked Tom intensely and undoubtedly resented the fact that George gave money to him and Christine. More importantly, George may well have had some serious conflicts about his alleged homosexual feelings, which one would not expect to be accepted calmly by the average man. At the same time that contact with Tom might have been sexually pleasurable for George, it might also have aroused stronger and stronger homosexual desires, producing ever greater conflicts. George was probably caught between the rewards and punishments of his situation in such a way that escape seemed difficult. We certainly do not suggest that George planned or consciously wished Tom's death, but the suicide did provide a solution to his problem.

REFERENCE

Weisman, A.D. and Kastenbaum, R. The psychological autopsy. *Community Mental Health Monograph* 4:1-59, 1968.

20

Preventing Suicide:
What Everyone Should Know

Because suicidal behavior can occur anywhere, anytime and to anyone, it is essential that everyone have, at the very least, a basic understanding of suicide, its warning signs and how to respond when confronted with a situation of this sort. Of course, some people are able to come to grips with their problems on their own, but most suicidal people want and need help from others to help solve their problems, or at least to help get through a suicidal crisis.

THE ROLE OF FAMILY AND FRIENDS

The most convenient and potentially most useful sources of help for the suicidal person are his friends and family. These people are usually available, they have considerable knowledge of the suicidal person's past history and it doesn't cost anything to talk to them. In addition, comfort and counsel from friends and relatives cannot be interpreted by the suicidal person as "paid friendship," as the relationship with a professional therapist sometimes is. If friends and relatives are sensitive to the behavior of the suicidal person and aware of the basic facts about suicide, they may be able to help save a life. There are a number of ideas that friends and families should keep in mind when dealing with potential suicides.

What To Do

If you believe that a person may be suicidal, there are steps you can take to help that person communicate his feelings to you. In addition to providing the potential suicide with an emotional outlet, you may also be able to help him with his problems and, at the same time, determine the degree of suicidal intent.

<u>Listen actively</u>. Suicidal people are often confused about what they want and how to get it. They have a need and they feel pain and they try to communicate these feelings to another person. Often they need help in clarifying confusing feelings. Sometimes this can be done by talking with them about their feelings (both those they express verbally and those they communicate by gestures or facial expressions). They may be able to better understand their own feelings simply by talking to someone and hearing themselves talk. Another way to help a person clarify his thoughts is by using the communication technique known as *active listening* (Gordon, 1970) or *empathic listening* (Carkhuff, 1969). Almost all hotline workers use this method when they speak to callers on the phone. In discussions with a suicidal person, the listener tries to understand what the sender is feeling or what his message means. The receiver restates the feelings inherent in the comments made by the potential suicide, feeding it back to him for verification. The receiver should not simply repeat the phrase or the objective facts that are mentioned, but instead should try to understand the implied feelings and then restate them. For example, the suicidal person might say, "I can't ever seem to get a date, and when I do, the girl is horrible. All girls are horrible and no nice girl will ever love me." The friend might respond to this by saying, "You'd like to have a girlfriend and you feel lonely without one, but you feel as if no nice girl will ever love you for who you are and you'll never have a good relationship." This response is stated in terms of the suicidal person's feelings, not in terms of the objective fact that there are plenty of "nice" girls. The receiver does not send back a message that contains his own opinions, questions or advice; he only feeds back his interpretation of what the suicidal person said. This process can ascertain that misunderstandings do not occur, a situation that often happens without the awareness of either party.

<u>Do not be afraid to ask direct questions</u> such as, "Do you feel so bad that you are considering suicide?" At one time or another, most people have considered suicide, even if it was just a fleeting thought. Do not worry that you might actually be giving the person the idea of committing suicide. In fact, bringing the subject out into the open can often be an enormous relief to the suicidal person who desperately wants to discuss his feelings and even specifically his suicidal plans, but is worried about scaring and alienating you. When you take the initiative and raise the question direct-

ly, it shows that you are taking the person seriously and that you are responding to his pain.

<u>Try to determine the degree of suicidal intent</u>. By asking a suicidal person questions about important issues, you will not only be able to determine the seriousness of his suicidal intent, but you will also encourage him to discuss his feelings. In addition, such questions let the potential suicide know that you are taking him seriously. If the answer is "Yes, I am considering suicide," you may ask him which method of suicide he is considering, does he have the means, has he decided when to do it and has he ever tried suicide before. The answers to these questions will allow you to determine the seriousness of his suicidal intent. You should also ask yourself how lethal is his plan, how available are the means and when you think he might act. Friends should not let social delicacy deter them from discussing specific details about suicidal behavior. It is a myth that talking about suicide to distressed individuals can encourage them to kill themselves. It is important to take the person's overall response into consideration when interpreting his answer; a very distressed person may say he is not suicidal even when he is. If you suspect this is the case, it may be helpful to ask him what he would do if he ever did feel suicidal.

<u>Do not leave the person alone if the level of suicidal intent seems very high</u>. If you believe that a person is seriously suicidal and may harm himself in the very near future, do *not* leave him alone. Even seemingly harmless activities, such as a trip to the bathroom, are opportunities for a person in the midst of a severe crisis to hurt himself.

<u>Seek professional help and follow through</u>. You will probably be able to most help the person if you do whatever you can to refer him to a professional for evaluation and treatment. Do not leave it up to him to seek help; follow through, not only by making sure that arrangements have been made to see someone, but also by making sure he gets there. Even if you are sworn to secrecy, remember that this is not a test of friendship but a cry for help. If you don't feel equipped to do this alone, find another person to help you or turn it over to someone else. If you don't know where to turn, look in the telephone directory for a 24-hour telephone counseling or suicide prevention service in your area. If the crisis is acute, call 911, a suicide hotline, or take the person to a hospital emergency room or a walk-in clinic at a psychiatric hospital.

What Not to Do

There are also certain things that you should avoid doing with a suicidal person.

Do not appear judgemental and do not beat around the bush. It is important to let the person know that you do not consider suicidal feelings cowardly or morally reprehensible and do not remind him of his obligations to his family and society. He is probably already overburdened with guilt and adding to it will not help. It is important to avoid euphemisms and be direct when you mention suicide. To ask, "Are you thinking of killing yourself?" is far more useful than to say, "You aren't thinking of doing something bad to yourself, are you?" The latter question invites potential suicides to lie and they may also conclude that you disapprove, not only of their feelings, but that you also disapprove of them. Finally, they will decide that you are not going to be able to help them and will, therefore, no longer discuss their feelings with you.

Never deny a suicidal person's feelings. His feelings are usually the basis of the problem. If a person says he feels worthless, it is not useful — in fact, it may be harmful — to tell him you don't agree. Even though you think it will make him feel better to hear you say, "Of course you're important; I love you and everyone else in the family feels the same way," you will not be helping him at all. The way you feel is not what concerns him. Most suicidal people are concerned with how they themselves feel, not how other people feel about them. Although, in reality, his worthlessness may not be an objective fact, it is a subjective reality for the person who believes it. Similarly, if a person says he wants to die, it is not useful to respond, "Oh, you don't really want to die — you're exaggerating." It may be true that their real goal may not be death, but they are using a convention of language to try to communicate the way they feel. When a potentially suicidal person is told that what he says or feels is not true, it may only make him think that you don't understand him. For these reasons, denial of feelings may actually be harmful and it certainly is not therapeutic.

Don't try to be a hero and "rescue" your suicidal friend or relative by assuming his problems and responsibilities and attempting to deal with the situation on your own. Professional help, which is available 24 hours a day, seven days a week, is never far away and people who are trained in suicide assessment and treatment are in a much better position than you to offer help to a person in a suicidal crisis.

PROFESSIONAL HELP

Although friends and family can be instrumental in aiding suicidal people, it must be recognized that there are times when this kind of intervention is not enough. For cases in which friends and relatives are themselves contributing to the disturbance that is causing a person distress and making him feel suicidal, the only person who may be able to offer help is someone outside of this tangle of unhappy relationships. As well, friends and relatives may be temperamentally unsuited to dealing with this kind of difficult problems; they may become impatient or agitated in spite of having the best intentions. They may even have reason to benefit from the person's suicide. Finally, a suicidal person may be seriously disturbed and in a state that cannot be addressed by a nonprofessional.

In such cases there are a number of resources to which potential suicides and those concerned about them can turn. First there are psychologists and other mental health professionals who can provide counseling and psychotherapy and psychiatrists who can prescribe appropriate medication. The majority of suicidal people are depressed and today there are a variety of effective antidepressants, such as Prozac for depressive disorders, and lithium for those with bipolar affective disorders (Schifano and De Leo, 1991). There are also effective short-term cognitive therapies for helping depressed suicidal clients (Freeman and Reinecke, 1993), as well as family therapy and group therapy for these clients and their families (Leenaars, Maltsberger and Neimeyer, 1994).

It is important to make sure that the professional you turn to for help is comfortable with the issue of suicide; many therapists do not like to deal with suicide cases and try to avoid accepting them as clients. The anxiety connected with the possibility of a client's suicide may be overwhelming for the therapist. If possible, therefore, it is wise to choose a therapist or counselor who has experience with suicidal people and who feels at ease accepting them as clients. Crisis intervention and suicide prevention centers can provide information about which therapists and counselors in the community are best suited for counseling suicidal clients.

In a 1989 study, Rutz and his colleagues in Sweden found that when family physicians (or general practitioners) were trained to recognize and treat depression and suicidal behavior, it led to a decrease in the local suicide rate. This illustrates the importance of training physicians and mental health professionals about suicide behavior and suicide prevention.

SUICIDE PREVENTION GROUPS AND CRISIS CENTERS

In most communities in the United States, and in Australia, Canada, the United Kingdom and western Europe, there are suicide organizations whose purpose is to prevent suicide and to advance its study. Generally, the goals of most of these organizations is to: support research projects that attempt to understand and treat depression; provide information and education about depression and suicide both to the general public, survivors and those plagued with depression and suicide; promote professional education for the recognition and treatment of depressed and suicidal individuals; publicize the magnitude of the problems of depression and suicide and the need for research, prevention and treatment; and to support programs for survivor treatment, research and education. Most of these organizations offer many different services, a general breakdown of which follows:

School Gatekeeper Training: This type of program is directed at school staff (teachers, counselors, coaches, etc.) to help identify students at risk of suicide and refer such students to appropriate help. These programs also teach staff how to respond to crises such as a sudden death of a classmate.

Community Gatekeeper Training: This type of gatekeeper program provides training to community members (clergy, police, merchants, recreation staff and physicians, nurses and other clinicians). This training is designed to help people identify at-risk youths and refer them as appropriate.

General Suicide Education: These programs provide students with facts about suicide, alert them to suicide warning signs and provide information on how to seek help for themselves and others. These programs often incorporated a variety of self-esteem or social competency development activities.

Screening Programs: Screening involves the administration of an instrument to identify high-risk youth in order to provide more targeted assessment and treatment. Repeated administration of the screening instrument can also be used to measure changes in attitudes or behavior over tiem, to test the effectiveness of an employed prevention strategy and to obtain early warning signs of potential suicidal behavior.

Peer Support Programs: These programs, which can be conducted in school or nonschool settings, are designed to foster peer relationships, competency development and social skills among youth at high risk of suicide.

Crisis Centers and Hotlines: These programs primarily provide telephone counseling for suicidal people. Hotlines are usually staffed by trained volunteers. Some of them also have a "drop in" crisis center and offer referrals.

Intervention after a Suicide: Strategies have been developed to cope with the potential crisis of suicide clusters that sometimes occur after a suicide occurs. They are designed in part to help prevent or contain suicide clusters and to help youth effectively cope with feelings of loss that come with the sudden death or suicide of a peer. Preventing further suicide is but one of the several goals of interventions made with friends and relatives of a suicide victim.

The Institute for Suicide Prevention in Santa Monica, California, a nonprofit organization founded in 1991 to help individuals dealing with the tragedy of suicide, offer a number of services including: Operation Reach-Out (a group of dedicated survivors who advertise the existence of the Institute); Youth Crisis Group; Drop-In Group; Survivors after Suicide Group; Young Adult Survivors; In-Service Training Workshops; and How You Can Help Group. One of the most important services offered is a 24-hour crisis counseling telephone hotline. San Francisco Suicide Prevention has a crisis line, a drug information line, a mental health information and referral line, an AIDS/HIV nightline and crisis line for Spanish-speaking callers. Most major cities have several local crisis counseling hotlines open 24 hours a day, so there is always someone to whom those in a crisis can turn.

These centers often operate in very different ways, but their members have in common a special regard for the problems of suicidal people and special training for dealing with them. In some countries, all the suicide prevention centers are administered and supervised by one group. In the United Kingdom, for example, all of the centers are run by an organization called The Samaritans, a nonreligious charity that has been offering emotional support to suicidal persons for over 40 years by phone, visit and letter. (The Samaritans are based in England, but they are an international organization.) They state that "callers are guaranteed absolute confidentiality and retain the right to make their own decisions including the decision to end their life." In the United States, each center is independent and although many meet the standards established by the American Association of Suicidology, there is no single model for how these centers operate.

The following is a description of how some suicide prevention centers operate. Funding for a suicide prevention center often comes from the local government or through grants from groups such as the United Way. In some cases, suicide centers are part of a larger mental health agency, such as a clinic or hospital. An administrative and professional staff often supervises the clinical work that is conducted by the counselors who may be therapists, psychologists, social workers or nonprofessional lay counselors and volunteers who are specially trained to assist suicidal people and their families. The primary service offered by most suicide prevention centers is a 24-hour telephone hotline, often advertised under different names such as suicide prevention, teen hotline, crisis intervention and problems in living. The rationale for crisis hotlines relies on the idea that suicide attempts are often precipitated by a stressful event, that they are often impulsive and are usually contemplated with ambivalence. Hotline counselors are designed to respond to the crisis, deter the caller from hurting himself and working with him until the crisis has passed. Hotlines offer an immediately available source of help; they do not require travel to a clinic; and they are anonymous, allowing callers the opportunity to be open without fear of harsh judgment.

At least one worker is always at the center to talk to the people who call in to discuss their problems. During the hours when demand is heavy, there may be four or five counselors available. Australia's Lifeline centers have a toll-free number. If all of the telephone counselors at one center are occupied with clients, the caller is automatically switched to an available counselor at a neighboring center. In some centers, a professional staff and trained lay counselors take the telephone calls during the day and volunteers take them in the evenings, at night and on weekends.

Some centers accommodate walk-in clients for face-to-face counseling and a number of them have established groups to help people who have attempted suicide as well as those who have lost a loved one to suicide (usually called survivors). Because the main purpose of these centers is to assist people in crisis, most of them do not take on clients for long-term therapy; to do so would tie up the counseling staff, making them unavailable for responding to new clients who are in crisis and need immediate help. Therefore, when clients seem to need long-term counseling, they are usually referred to other agencies in the community or the surrounding area.

Telephone counselors are trained to use many of the same techniques for dealing with suicidal people that were recommended earlier in this chapter for the family and friends. Their principal aim is to help callers come to grips with their own feelings, reach their own solutions to their problems and above all, to help them get through a suicidal crisis without hurting themselves. The techniques they use to guide the callers' thinking in a constructive direction are the reflection of feelings and the asking of questions at appropriate times. Hotline counselors are not hesitant to discuss the difficult issue of suicide and they are able to talk very directly about the callers' desire to die. As pointed out earlier, many psychotherapists are very ill at ease with suicidal clients and fear that they will be at fault if their clients complete suicide. This anxiety is partly due to the fact that most therapists see relatively few clients who are suicidal and therefore have little experience in this area. Telephone counselors, after working with large numbers of suicidal clients, soon become well acquainted with the issues involved. They acquire a vast fund of experience in working with suicidal and distressed clients and so become quite skilled in helping them.

Being a telephone crisis counselor is a very difficult and often stressful job. Clients can always break off contact by hanging up, and so it is very important for counselors to make sure that their timing is good and that they listen and communicate carefully. Counselors must also try to get necessary information from clients who are crying uncontrollably or unable to talk coherently. Clients sometimes bring a great deal of suspicion to the telephone encounter, often repeatedly demanding to know whether the telephone line is tapped and whether the counselor is qualified to do therapy. Also, counselors may have to handle several calls simultaneously, meaning that they will have to ask some clients to hold the line, or call back later, while they talk to others who may seem to be in more desperate shape. Clearly this takes enormous skill and careful assessment of each caller.

If clients are in a severely suicidal state and say that they have a loaded gun or have already taken pills or have cut themselves, telephone counselors may decide that the situation demands more active intervention. Only a very few centers have staff available who can leave the center (or their homes) to go to a client in acute crisis; most centers do not allow this. Films and television movies often show a crisis hotline worker calling the police to ask them to go to the rescue of a person who may have attempted suicide. In real life, this kind of action is rarely taken. Some municipalities forbid their police officers to force their way into a home unless a crime has been committed — and suicide is not a crime. Therefore, in most cases, when the police are called, the suicidal person must admit them into his home. In these cases, not only must the person be physically able to open the door, but he must also consent to police intervention. Furthermore, when a suicide prevention center asks the police to break into a home because they suspect that a suicide has been committed and the police find that no seriously life-threatening act has occurred, it may cause them to distrust future requests made by the center. Sometimes counselors decide that even though a person may have committed a seriously suicidal action, the serious danger is over and the person is stable enough to go to the hospital alone. As a case in point, one night a woman called a suicide prevention center in which I was working and she told me that she had cut her wrists. After talking to her for an hour and deciding that she seemed to be emotionally stable and that she wasn't weakening physically, I decided against sending the police to her rescue.

Interestingly, very few of the calls made to suicide prevention centers are actually concerned with suicidal preoccupations. (It is important to note, however, that even though a caller does not discuss suicide, it does not mean that he is not suicidal.) Many clients want to try to resolve a problem or decide on a course of action and simply want someone to talk to. Some callers have chronic problems and call regularly to discuss their situation. These "chronic callers" may call back hundreds of times and may become so well-known to the staff that the counselors worry when they don't hear from them. Chronic callers usually use the service to simply vent their feelings rather than to get support during a crisis. If these chronic callers were not able to get this kind of support from the telephone hotline workers, chances are good that their problems could build up and turn into major ones, perhaps requiring professional therapy.

If a counselor decides that telephone counseling is not appropriate for a client, there are a number of other resources that are available. Counselors may refer clients to a specialist (e.g., a physician, a lawyer or a group such as Planned Parenthood); they may suggest that the client go to a mental health clinic for face-to-face therapy; or they may advise the client to contact a psychiatrist or psychologist for long-term psychotherapy. Most suicide prevention centers have good relationships with the other mental health facilities in the community and can often arrange for clients to be seen immediately by other professionals rather than have them put on a waiting list. Even when a prevention center refers clients elsewhere, they often work out a coordinated treatment plan with the referred party. Clients often continue to call in and talk to telephone counselors whenever they feel the need.

The following is a list of the larger suicide prevention organizations, all of which also maintain Internet sites:

- American Association of Suicidology
- The American Foundation for Suicide Prevention
- SPAN Suicide Prevention Advocacy Network
- SA\VE Suicide Awareness\Voices of Education
- National Mental Health Association
- The Samaritans
- International Association for Suicide Prevention
- National Mental Health Association
- Canadian Association for Suicide Prevention

SCHOOL SUICIDE AND DEATH EDUCATION PROGRAMS

In recent years, many school systems have incorporated death education and suicide intervention and prevention programs into their curricula (Stevenson and Stevenson, 1996), a development that is, in large part, in response to the enormous rise in adolescent suicide in the past few decades. Many of these programs can assist parents who need help (for their children or themselves), often by referring them to appropriate agencies and support groups in the area. Many people and groups have criticized these programs because they feel that they upset students who are depressed and possibly suicidal and that they are not able to prevent suicide (Shaffer et al., 1988). Others believe that the programs are important and have been successful in achieving their goals (Ryerson, 1991). Unfortunately, aside from the educational programs for school students, little other effort has been made to inform the general public about suicide. Perhaps as more and more people become aware of the pervasiveness and seriousness of the problem, they will seek out information on their own and make sure they learn how to respond to suicidal behavior. It is precisely for this reason that this book has been written.

THE INTERNET

Fortunately, there is now a good deal of information available on the Internet that is immediately available to anyone with a computer. Almost all of the suicide and crisis intervention organizations have websites whose varied offerings include: excellent and detailed information on critical issues such as warning signs, what to do and what not to do when faced with a person's suicidal crisis; answers to frequently asked questions; phone numbers of crisis hotlines and addresses of organizations; a comprehensive listing of support groups in your community and on the Internet; links to more specific information; and listings of useful books, articles and journals. Some of them even offer online counseling, many of them respond daily to Email letters and there are also quite a few electronic self-help support groups where people can talk to each other about their suicidal feelings, thoughts, intentions or previous attempts in a safe, emotionally supportive environment. Other Internet resources are mailing lists and newsgroups which are forums of discussion for people who work in or who are interested in the fields of suicide prevention and crisis counseling, or who themselves are suicidal. The following is a list of valuable Internet resources and their website addresses:

• Suicide: Read This First
   www.geocities.com/RainForest/1801/suicide1

This site is intended for those who are seriously contemplating suicide in the immediate future. It is unique because the author of the site speaks bluntly yet compassionately to the intended reader (i.e., the suicidal person) and asks him to make a pact with himself to allow a waiting period before acting upon any thoughts of suicide. This is a very special page that could very possibly help those in a crisis.

• Suicide Awareness — Voices of Education
   www.save.org

A popular site, SA\VE's mission is to educate people about suicide and to help and speak out for suicide survivors. The site offers background information on suicide, suggestions on what to do if someone is suicidal, a reviewed book list and discussion of the grief that follows any suicide.

• Suicide Information and Education Centre
   www.siec.ca

SIEC is the largest English-language suicide information resource center and library in the world. Established in 1982, the SIEC collection contains more than 20,000 print and audiovisual materials on all aspects of suicidal behavior. In addition, SIEC contains an excellent state-by-state listing of crisis centers across the United States and Canada complete with both business and hot-line numbers.

• American Foundation for Suicide Prevention
  www.afsp.org

Originally called the American Suicide Foundation, The American Foundation for Suicide Prevention is dedicated to the advancement of suicide research and prevention. In addition to offering financial support to many suicide research projects, the foundation also provides the general public with up-to-date information on depression and suicide. This site includes a searchable database of crisis centers and allows the user to access recent suicide research findings.

• San Francisco Suicide Prevention
  www.sf.suicide.org

Founded in 1963, the SFSP is one of the oldest volunteer crisis hotlines in the U.S. Their services are provided 24 hours a day by over 250 trained volunteers. This well-designed site is geared toward anyone who is interested in suicidal behavior. It offers an excellent "what you can do" section that is full of good advice and gives facts about suicide, its warning signs, prevention measures and things to pay attention to when assessing suicidal risk.

• The Samaritans
  www.samaritans.org.uk

One of the largest suicide prevention organizations in the world, the Samaritans' primary aim is to befriend people in a suicidal crisis 24 hours a day, 7 days a week. They can be contacted in a number of ways, including Email, telephone, text telephone (for the deaf) and regular mail, and they offer counseling to walk-ins. In addition, they have a toll free telephone service that is available to members of the armed forces. The Samaritans are part of an enormous worldwide organization called Befrienders International, which has branches throughout the world (including Zimbabwe, Russia, Egypt, Japan, Barbados, Brazil, Malaysia and Poland), each one of which is listed by name, phone number and address.

• Dr. John Grohol's Mental Health Page (Psych Central)
  www.coil.com/~grohol

With one of the most well maintained sites on the web, Dr.
Grohol covers everything from autism to depression and suicide.
Not only does Dr. Grohol review many other websites and print
publications, but he also provides links to suicide resources on
his "Suicide Helpline" page. With features like a weekly "real
time" chat hour, it's easy to see why hundreds of thousands of
people have visited this page. Dr. Grohol will respond quickly
via Email to any questions he receives.

• Growth House, Inc.
  www.Growthhouse.org

Because of its comprehensive offering of hypertext links and
reviews and ratings of other sites, this is an excellent starting
place for everyone interested in learning more about suicide and
other issues pertaining to death and bereavement.

SURVIVORS OF SUICIDE

Understandably, the suicide of a friend or family member is
extremely difficult to come to terms with. The death of a loved one
by any means is hard to handle, but a suicide is especially difficult,
painful and complicated for survivors. Even though the general
perception in society that suicide has "bad" connotations is not as
prevalent as it used to be, it still exists and, therefore, many people
find it difficult to admit to others that a loved one has died by his
own hand. Survivors may be afraid that others will judge them
harshly, that they will think there was something "wrong" within
their family. Stigmatized and rejected, survivors of suicide are often
hesitant to admit the real cause of death. This may cause survivors
to withdraw and isolate themselves, resulting in a lack of important
support systems.

Death by suicide is often violent and bloody. Finding a loved one
after he has shot himself in the head or finding him hanging and
having to cut down his body may scar a family member for life,
causing him severe anxiety, frightening memories and nightmares
and other symptoms of post-traumatic stress. Also, many survivors
feel abandoned and rejected because they believe the decedent will-
ingly chose to separate from them, a thought that causes terrible
pain for many suicide survivors.

Survivors often feel an excessive amount of guilt and anger.

Sometimes they obsess on questions of "what if" and thoughts of "if only." Constant review of the events that led up to the suicide often leaves the survivor convinced that he could have done something if he had only, for example, paid more attention or, even worse, hadn't argued that day. For some survivors, the need to determine why the suicide occurred in the first place eclipses the bereavement process and becomes an obsession. Unfortunately, this quest is often in vain because the real answer can only be given by the person who killed himself. Sometimes survivors direct their feelings of guilt at other people, blaming the rest of the world for the suicide and their pain. When this happens, it often serves to prevent their ability to accept help from other people.

Finally, because of feelings of abandonment, survivors often have a hard time trusting others. They don't want to become close to someone and have the same thing happen again. Combined with the typical lack of support from sources who would ordinarily be there to talk, listen and comfort in the event of a different kind of death, survivors of suicide are often in a very lonely and painful situation.

While not everyone needs treatment, if grief symptoms are unusual and lingering (severe depression and guilt, self-blame and suicidal thoughts), treatment is probably indicated. There are a variety of treatment options for survivors of suicide such as one-on-one, family and group therapy. Also, in the last few decades, support groups for survivors of suicide have been established in communities all over the world that offer friends and families support and information in a nonjudgmental environment. Most major cities now have support groups for survivors and there are also several national organizations devoted to the cause. As well, there are several electronic support groups that offer emotional support to survivors who are distressed and want to discuss and begin to resolve their problems stemming from the suicide of a loved one. The American Association of Suicidology publishes a newsletter for survivors of suicide, and many of the sessions at its annual conference are concerned with survivor issues. Finally, the importance of these groups extends beyond offering support to survivors; because the risk of suicide is increased in survivors, it is important for them to have a good understanding of suicide, its causes and its effects.

RESTRICTING ACCESS TO METHODS FOR SUICIDE

Because impulsiveness appears to play an important role in suicide (especially among young people), and because ambivalence is a typical characteristic of suicides (i.e., the decision to go through with the act waxes and wanes), many suicide prevention specialists argue that if lethal means are not readily available when a person decides to attempt suicide, it may affect the outcome in several ways. First, it may delay the attempt, allowing the person to later decide against suicide. Second, it may prompt the person to use a less lethal means, therefore allowing for a greater chance that he may be saved. Furthermore, there is the possibility that some attempts would never be acted on if substantial effort was needed to arrange for the method of suicide.

We can see what happens when lethal means are restricted by the following incident. In England, in the 1960s and 1970s, during the time that the domestic gas industry switched from coal gas (containing highly toxic carbon monoxide) to natural gas (containing less toxic methane), the English suicide rate declined by about 30 percent. This suggests that many people who would have used gas to kill themselves apparently did not switch to another method when their preference became unavailable.

The emission controls on cars, instituted to reduce pollution, have also made exhaust fumes less toxic and therefore less likely to cause death. Another way to make it harder for people to poison and kill themselves with carbon monoxide from cars would be for manufacturers to install a device that would automatically turn off the engine after it idled for a few minutes. Also, to make it harder to attach a hose to the exhaust pipes of cars, manufacturers could change the shape of the pipes from round to flat and wide.

Clarke and Lester (1989) documented the many ways in which easy access to lethal methods for suicide, such as firearms, increases their use for suicide. They urged such tactics as placing limits on the sale and ownership of firearms; fencing in bridges and high buildings from which people jump; restricting the availability of poisonous fertilizers and insecticides in developing countries where they are often used to commit suicide; as well as reducing the number of pills that doctors prescribe and the prescription of less toxic medications.

It would seem particularly important to restrict ready access to firearms. Nearly two-thirds of all suicides among males aged 15 to 24 are committed with guns. Unlike drug ingestion and carbon monoxide poisoning, a suicide attempt with a firearm is often immediately lethal, leaving very little opportunity for rescue.

Critics have argued that if people have trouble obtaining the means of first choice for suicide, they will simply find another method. Clarke and Lester replied that many suicidal people have a specific preferred method for suicide and would not switch. If they do switch, they may have to use a less lethal method. Furthermore, because the suicidal state is often a crisis state that can pass in a very short while, if it is difficult for a person to quickly find a lethal alternative, by the time he finally obtains the means for committing suicide, the suicidal crisis may be past.

The strategy of restricting access to methods for committing suicide is frequently used in hospitals and prisons to prevent patients and inmates from taking their lives. A great deal of thought has been given to how to make rooms and cells "suicide-proof" (Lester and Danto, 1993). In correctional facilities, not only should surveillance be intensified for inmates who seem suicidal, but also every effort should be made to restrict suicidal inmates' access to dangerous items that could be used for suicide.

Restricting access to lethal methods would not necessarily reduce suicide attempts, but it certainly has the potential for preventing suicides.

WHY PREVENT SUICIDE?

In the same way that most people believe that the prolongation of life is always desirable over death, most people also assume that the prevention of suicide is always the right avenue of thought. Most people regard life as sacred. Reverence for life is a part of many religions; even when it is separated from theological tenets, this belief remains deeply ingrained in most everyone. A murderer is looked upon with horror, and the people who deny the importance of life by killing themselves are often considered insane or evil. The taboo against taking one's own life is so deeply ingrained that the direct discussion of suicide is often avoided. This avoidance may extend even to the distortion of the actual cause of death on a suicide's death certificate.

In addition to these deep-rooted feelings about the value of life, there are many objective reasons for preventing suicide. Persons whose suicide attempts are thwarted are often grateful for being saved, and they shudder at the idea that they might actually have died. Those who call a suicide prevention center are clearly ambivalent about dying or else they wouldn't have called; they are asking for alternative solutions to their problem. If a person commits suicide, his survivors usually suffer terribly. Not only are they deprived of the companionship and perhaps the financial support of their loved one, but they may also experience great guilt and distress because they are afraid that they contributed to the suicide's problems or at least failed to save him. In cultures where suicide is considered highly taboo, the family may feel disgraced. Children whose parent commits suicide may be tormented by the notion that they might have inherited suicidal tendencies.

Finally, many people choose suicide as a solution to problems in their lives and they see death as the only way to escape when in actuality there are other ways of coping. If we save them, we can give them another chance to work through their difficulties. The successful and permanent prevention of suicide involves correction of the problems that are leading people toward suicide, thus making them happier and more productive, rather than simply keeping them alive.

In spite of all these good reasons for the prevention of suicide, the question sometimes arises whether it is appropriate to try to prevent the suicide in all circumstances. Many suicidologists would say that prevention efforts are always appropriate. Existentialists, on the other hand, would contend that suicide may sometimes be a healthy act. In 1958, Binswanger, an existential psychiatrist, said of one of his patients that he believed that suicide was the only healthy, free, mature and responsible action she could take. Most suicide experts would not go so far as to advocate suicide because of its existential advantages. However, when a person is seriously preoccupied with suicide for a long period of time and therefore requires constant observation and guarding (perhaps in the locked ward of a psychiatric hospital), we must ask ourselves whether compromising his dignity and humanity is not more damaging to the quality of his life as a whole than the possibility that his life will end in suicide.

This issue is especially relevant today because more and more people who are suffering from chronic terminal illnesses such as AIDS are deciding that they would rather die by suicide than live a life with so much suffering. There are books in print that explain how to kill oneself quickly and relatively painlessly (Humphry, 1991) and physicians who are willing to help (Kevorkian, 1988). Dr. Kevorkian has even designed a poison-dispensing "suicide machine" for people who want to die. Some people rationally decide to commit suicide, feeling that death (both subjectively and objectively) is preferable to further life. In certain circumstances, suicide may appear to be the best possible solution to an impossible situation. As people have different styles of life, so each, it could be argued, should have the right to his own style of death. For some individuals, death by suicide may be the most appropriate end to life.

In strong disagreement, Shneidman and his colleagues (1965) argued that even severely ill persons should be discouraged from committing suicide because "while there is life, there is hope" and also because their deaths will cause so much guilt in survivors. Similarly, Richman (1993) feels that rather than acquiescing in the suicidal deaths of patients with chronic and terminal illnesses, we should make strenuous efforts to improve the quality of their final months or years of life.

In response to Shneidman's point, it is rather rare for a person approaching death to be totally cured and able to return to a normal life. And as for the guilt of relatives, it would be more realistic to say that guilt should be experienced by those who insist on forcing a loved one to maintain an unwanted and painful life. A survivor's severe guilt over the suicide of a gravely ill relative may be pathological or deserved because he treated that person unfairly. In either case, the guilt is not an event within the life of the dying person and he is the one who should be our chief concern.

We should realize that the quality of life can sometimes be more important than its quantity. There are times when people should not be subjected to prolonged agony followed by inevitable death simply on the grounds that no matter what, "life is sacred."

REFERENCES

Binswanger, L. The case of Ellen West. In R. May, E. Angel and H.F. Ellenberger (eds.), *Existence*. New York: Basic Books, 1958.

Carkhuff, R.R. Helping and human relations. New York: Holt, Rinehart and Winston, 1969.

Clarke, R.V. and Lester, D. Suicide: *Closing the Exits*. New York: Springer-Verlag, 1989.

Freeman, A. and Reinecke, M.A. *Cognitive Therapy of Suicide Behavior*. New York: Springer, 1993.

Gordon, T. *Parent Effectiveness Training*. New York: Wyden, 1970.

Humphry, D. *Final Exit*. Eugene, OR: Hemlock Society, 1991.

Kervorkian, J. The last taboo. *Medicine and Law* 7:1-44, 1988.

Leenaars, A.A., Maltsberger, J.T., and Neimeyer, R.A. (eds.). *Treatment of Suicidal People*. Washington, DC: Taylor and Francis, 1994.

Lester, D. The effectiveness of suicide prevention centers. *Suicide & Life-Threatening Behavior* 23:263-267, 1993.

Lester, D. and Danto, B.L. *Suicide Behind Bars: Prediction and Prevention*: Philadelphia: The Charles Press, 1993.

Lukas, C. and Seiden, H.M. *Silent Grief*. New York: Scribner's, 1987.

Richman, J. *Preventing Elderly Suicide*. New York: Springer, 1993.

Ryerson, D. Suicide awareness education in schools. In A.A.

Leenaars and S. Wenckstern (eds.), *Suicide Prevention in Schools.* New York: Hemisphere, 1991.

Schifano, F. and De Leo, D. Can pharmacological intervention aid in the prevention of suicidal behavior? *Pharmacopsychiatry* 24:113-117, 1991.

Shaffer, D., Garland, A., Gould, M., Fisher, P. and Trautman, P. Preventing teenage suicide. *Journal of the American Academy of Child and Adolescent Psychiatry* 27:675-687, 1988.

Shneidman, E.S., Farberow, N.L. and Leonard, C.V. *Some Facts about Suicide.* Washington, DC: U.S. Government Printing Office, 1965.

Stevenson, R. and Stevenson, E. (eds). *Teaching Students about Death: A Comprehensive Guide for Educators and Parents.* Philadelphia: The Charles Press, 1996.

Index